The Genesis Touch

A Study in Biblical Theology

A Love Story

By Judy Weerstra

Dedicated to

Hans M. Weerstra,
Southwest CTR for World Mission
This entire work is a product of the love and patience granted to me by my husband (missionary and apostle) who painstakingly worked with me to form a holistic, spiritual, charismatic, and orthodox Christian theology in cooperation with the work and illumination of the Holy Spirit. It is the product of our intense desire to see the Body of Christ become theologically, spiritually, and missiological mature to reach the nations. Though I was Han's prophet, and spokesman, nevertheless, "He still speaks."

Dr. Daniel P. Fuller,
Fuller Theological Seminary
This unassuming professor of theology at my alma mater irrevocably changed my mind, heart, and will toward radical obedience to Christ through the first five chapters of his book, "*Unity of the Bible.*" The profound effect his teaching and thinking have had upon my life and future is inestimable. I am grateful for his faithfulness to endure persecution and often obscurity, both are marks of a true saint. Thank you, Dr. Fuller. I pray you will forgive me for taking your findings in a completely different direction as a "new Calvinist."

Jim and Linda Warren,
Former missionaries
For all their hard work in editing the many drafts of this book, without which this current book would have not existed. Thank You!

The First Class

"For me, this course has been like eating at this incredible banqueting table of the Lord. The content has been of the finest delicacies of bread ad wine, but the family that has shared and partaken has been of a royal family. I would highly recommend it to all Christians and non-Christians." **Debbie Martin**

"The things which I know to be true in my spirit were confirmed in my mind through the Scriptures. I now have understanding in my mind for the glory in my heart. Thank you so much!" **Dawn Damant**

"God is shedding light on His Word in these last days and this course is one of His brightest beams! 'In his light, we shall see light!' I know the impact of this course has only begun in my life, and I've been following the Lord Jesus for 45 years. You will love its "grist!"
Patti LaVenture

"The class was SO beneficial to me, now affecting more the way I see God's holiness and love [benevolent]! Especially who He is as three in one. [There were so] many revelations, before, during, and after. I see so much growth for me!" **Robert Gable**

"More than any other Bible study or teaching I've received, The Genesis Touch has helped me to begin to understand and see the Bible as a Unity. The Genesis Touch gives and enables us to understand Bible events in time and space. No study has revealed Jesus Christ as the central figure and subject of the Genesis Touch. Without hesitation, I recommend this. May God use it to open your soul's door to the Light of Him who is Love. "**Gene Atkinson**

About the Authors and Editor

Hans Weerstra (Editor) was born in the Netherlands and raised as a member of a Christian family who participated in the Dutch Underground movement for the protection of Christian and Jews during the reign of Hitler and the Nazi Regime during WWII. Dr. Weerstra's family was awarded special recognition by the Israeli government and awarded a tree in the Garden of the Righteous Gentiles for their work in hiding Jews. They were also awarded special immigration status by President Eisenhower to enter the United States for their work in the Allied Underground Resistance.

Dr. Weerstra lived for twenty years among the indigenous peoples of southern Mexico. He holds a D.Miss from Fuller Theological Seminary, and Th.M from Calvin Seminary, Grand Rapids, MI. He was a missionary for over 40 years. He was the editor of the International Journal of Frontier Missions and the director of the Southwest Center of Frontier Missions, in El Paso, Texas. Dr. Weerstra passed away in April of 2011 in El Paso, Texas.

Judy Weerstra (author) was born in El Paso, Texas, She has an undergraduate degree in World History, English, and Teaching. She worked with indigenous peoples in Juarez Mexico. She and her husband taught Spanish with Youth With A Mission for 7 years before moving to Pasadena to work on the Perspectives on the World Christian Movement with Dr. Ralph Winter. Mrs. Weerstra graduated from Fuller Theological Seminary in 1992 with a degree in Missiology.

INTRODUCTION

The opening account of Genesis is possibly the most famous line of Scripture. Its truth resonates across cultures. It has become poetry for the West and yet few understand what it means. When the narrative is maintained it spells out a story of grandeur and majesty that makes even a cold-hearted person bend the knee. Although it's a story that we've heard so many times, (even from the moon) that we tend to leave it at that beautiful and poetic level. But the Genesis Touch takes every word seriously and in doing so discovers themes that are virtually undiscoverable without a guide.

Although the Genesis Touch is a return to the basic principles of worldview, i.e., notions of life and death, sin and evil, it is also the disclosure of God's plan for the ages given with a fresh perspective, known as Biblical Theology. Our rationale for reinstating biblical theology comes from Luke 24:27 where Jesus opened the Scriptures, "And beginning with Moses and the Prophets, [Jesus] explained to [the disciples] what was said in all the Scriptures concerning Himself." He began with Genesis and continued to the Prophets. We see this process in biblical theology as a development of a "love story" between God and man. This is not only a primer for new believers but food for mature Christians. Every line of Scripture has meaning and we unwrap the enigma of Genesis in this volume. Enjoy and may God bless you as you take the journey with us.

Chapter One

THE MYSTERY OF GOD

1.1 GOD AS BEING

The first and only mover in the opening chapter of Genesis is God. Nothing explains who or how He came into existence because as His name tells us, I AM has always existed. Very early on He tells us that He always was, is, and will be; in this manner, He reveals to us His eternal existence also known as His aseity.

At the burning bush, Moses asks God, "What is your name and whom shall I say sent me?" God replies, "I am who I am, tell them the I AM sent you" (Ex. 3:14,15). It's a term of blunt reality: "It is what it is" as the common expression goes. "I AM," or *"hayah"* means "To be, To arise, to exist, and Life."

He is saying, I, AM. I AM Life. I AM Being, present everywhere and have an immediate perception of all things. He is also saying, "I have always existed, and I will always exist." Hebrew is a language of action, dynamic and experiential, there is nothing passive in this name. His name is not an idea but a term for ONGOING LIFE. God goes on to tell Moses, "This is my eternal name, my name to remember for all generations" (Ex.3:15-16). God is outside of time and space with no beginning and without end. This is known as His eternality. All things begin with Him. Our earth, the heavens, and everything we see, hear and experience were created by Him. There is nothing that exists or has existed that did not originate from within His mind or without His power. He creates knowledge, time, love, and catastrophe. All reality lies within His dominion.

1.2 GOD AS PERSON

The intriguing thing about God is that He is a Person, in dramatic contradiction to the gods of this world; or ideas of the Omnipotent such as Fate, Karma, Allah, Brahim, or the many tribal deities of man. These are impersonal forces in life. The fact that God identifies himself as a person is impossible to ignore. Foremost, there is the use of the first person pronoun in His self-revelation. He identifies Himself as an "I." Second, He communicates with us, speaking directly to our minds through our everyday language. Every man hears him in his/her native tongue. His communication reveals that nothing can be hidden from His sight. Third, He thinks, feels, and wills, three attributes that characterize Personhood. Fourth, He possesses self-consciousness which is completely at His disposal. He never has to wonder why he did something or said something. He is not a mystery to himself as we sometimes are. He is a God—Person. What is that? We need to take those terms on their own to understand Him.

What is a god?

There is a difference between "a god" and "The God." The first is one among many, and the second is the Highest God of whom there is not equal. The Highest God possesses ultimate power without any limitations, maintains His identity and power without any outside agency, has ultimate knowledge of all things, and should be worshipped for what He has created. He is separate from what He has created, possesses endless life, and cannot die. These are features of the Absolute God. The Christian God possesses attributes of both the absolute God and the attributes of a Person. He fixed Himself from all eternity with unity and diversity within Himself. He's not numerically diverse but egocentrically differentiated. It would be like saying there was one person with three separate frontal cortex regions, each one thinking independently of the others, yet one Person.

With the existence of three frontal cortex regions or the "governing regions of the brain," one person would make known His will initiating a plan, one would render judgment on such plan, and the other would execute the said plan *if* it was the highest form of wisdom and consistent with God's majesty, dignity, and intelligence. The Godhead possesses an internal council that can govern the nature of reality, the cosmos, and ultimately the plan of humanity. This definition begs the question: Can someone with those attributes possibly be a person?

What is a person?

What does it mean to be a person? What attributes are necessary? Ancient sources have always understood "personhood" as synonymous with the word "face," the face being the core or central part of a man's "essence." Another word that was frequently used was "countenance." In Numbers 6:24-26, "The Lord bless you and keep you; The Lord make His *face* shine upon you, and be gracious to you; The Lord lift His *countenance* upon you and give you peace." Ps. 27:9 says, "Do not hide your *face* from me...." These are terms by which we recognize the features of personhood in the divine. However, a modern definition and perhaps a greater understanding of personhood is seen in the agreement between science and religion that personhood implies self-consciousness or awareness of "me" from an awareness of what is "not me." In agreement with this premise, the attribute of "thinking" or "mind" involves making distinctions between what the mind perceives as "us" from what is "not us." Personhood makes necessary an "other."

To have self-consciousness, there must be another self.

Helpful to this discussion is one scholar's view, "The self is mutually constituted with the presence of another" such as a mother, father, or friend (Adrian Carr). In other words, one cannot exist without an "other"; they are born together as twin components of man's unique creation. This idea lies at the base of "man as a social being." Many experiments have been conducted in this field of selfhood which conclusively prove this statement: Man cannot live in isolation. Man's self-perception is initially formed by others (at least one). Unless Adam had God to relate to, he could not have had a sufficient sense of himself to be aware of his existence. This lack of "other" (profound isolation) is the basis for a mental breakdown. The human mind cannot perceive itself and by necessity must create "another." The greater the isolation the greater the emotional and psychological damage of an individual. Think of the movie "Castaway" with Tom Hanks. The fact that Hanks's character had to create another person, i.e., "Wilson," shows that this "friendship" kept him sane. Hanks's character divided himself into two people to "experience" himself, without which he would have gone psychotic. Wilson became so real to him that when he eventually lost sight of him in the ocean, he grieved, as though Wilson had become a real person.

Hindu scholars say that personhood cannot be ascribed to the infinite because personhood necessitates at least two people. Continuing, the Hindus say their idea of Brahman (their term for god is one without attributes) is closer to the true concept of God. They say that God cannot be described by any known features. Brahman IS, but they do not know how *it* is, only that *it* is. Notice the impersonal pronoun. For the Hindu, Brahman, or God, is infinite and all-encompassing and cannot be directly perceived because the finite cannot apprehend or surround the infinite; nevertheless, they claim that there is an intuitive knowledge that Brahman exists. It is like saying that the ant cannot fully perceive the elephant because the ant can never circumvent the mass of the elephant; therefore, the ant cannot know what the elephant fully is, only that *it* exists.

The Hindus say that without this duality God could not be both God and Person. They claim anyone with infinite attributes cannot be a Person, since persons have limitations imposed on them by the presence of another being. It creates in humans a sense of self that only exists in the community. Without another person, the "I" become diffused and holds no meaning. If everything is me, then what is me? A "god" has none of these issues so God must be in everything (pantheism). Professor Hodge answers this Hindu objection by saying,

> The need for another is met within the plurality of God. There is a second person to whom the Father relates. He says, "We know that according to the Scriptures and the faith of the Church universal, there are in the unity of the Godhead three distinct persons, the Father, the Son, and the Holy Spirit; so that from [all] eternity, the Father can say, 'I,' and the Son, 'Thou'" [Hodge, I, 392].

With a council of wise minds within Himself, He could view Himself objectively. The existence of another person gave Him a sense of His own character and holiness. The Glory Presence maintains boundaries within Himself so that He is not diffused, fluid, and non-personal, but within Himself, there is both self and other, and it results that everything outside of Himself is within His power to rule or govern

1.3 GOD AS PLURAL YET ONE

The great *Shema* of the Old Testament in Dt. 6:4 says, "Hear O. Israel! The Lord is our God, the Lord is One!" The *Hebrew Chaldean Dictionary* says that the word for "one" *(Echad S 259)* represents an ordinal number, having the meaning of first as well as a "collective" or "unity." Ordinal numbers tell the order of things in a set—first, second, third, etc. Ordinal numbers do not show quantity. They only show rank. It carries the designation of "first" or the "principal" as in all things have their origin in this principle, the First One, or the First Cause. The word "one" *(Echad S 259)* is also used in "day one" of Genesis 1:1 which means that this day stands alone in its position in contrast to all the other days.

The *Shema* could easily be saying that God is the First Cause, the Prime Mover, the First Principle, whose revelation unfolds to us in a temporal sense. The *Schema* could be read, "Hear O. Israel, the Lord is First Above All Beings." John 17:3 gives a hint of this usage when Jesus prayed the high priestly prayer "...that they may be one, as we are one" signifying that we are to make God, "...the chief person in our lives and put Him first in all things" and we are to be wholly given over to God in all three aspects of our being, the mind, the emotions, and the will.

There is a secondary meaning to the word *"Echad"* (S 259). God's "oneness" is also a qualitative union not just a number in order of importance but it also describes a state of being, one which states that within this union each person possesses His personality, that is, able to think independently of the others yet in such complete unity that they can be considered one—this is their divine simplicity. It can be described as one in essence. According to His Name, I AM, God has always existed as a three-fold being, three unified centers (being) of consciousness, each with equal powers, attributes, and yet individualized personalities. They are perfectly unified in love and purpose. If one is good, then all are good because they are of the same substance. The degree of unity is so strong that they always refer to themselves as one even though they possess individuality. God is not alone but exists in such a way to have inner counsel at his disposal within Himself.

1.4 MUST GOD BE A PERSON TO BE LOVE?

Since love by nature exceeds the singular "I" dimension and enters into the "thou," we say that love by necessity demands an "other" (Hodge, 1 392). Affections must have an object says Erickson, "Love, to be love, must have both a subject and an object" (221). There must be another self that can be loved. To say, "God is love," implies a relationship otherwise there would be no point to this attribute. It is a personal and relational term. The question is, "If God did not possess personhood could He be love?" The answer is no. God must "by necessity" not only be a person but at least two people. These two must also be so unified that they are considered one.

What does love require?

For love to be satisfying there must be equality in substance and power. While it is true that one can love one's dog, cat, or even places and things a great deal, and we know of such cases, we also know that kind of love can never be fully satisfying. Love must be reciprocated in equal measure (whole heart, mind, and soul) between two people or it can never be fully satisfying. No matter how much I love my dog, it can never be my intellectual and emotional equal. The love between persons and animals will always be of a lower order than the love between persons.

This quote is pertinent to the discussion,

> *Love, it is agreed must have an object; it never permits itself to be solitary. Love ceases to exist if it does not pour forth the ardor of its affections, and yet the object of love must be upon something equal in station to itself. If a man recognizes his own dignity, then he will not attach himself to things inferior, for fear of injuring his love. Thus the soul learns that it must not cannot, seek a love that is either solitary or degrading, for should it do this, its love will cease. The goal is now known, seek a love that will be yours alone and also one that is especially worthy. (McGill, 220)*

"This kind of love," says Dr. Erickson, "is necessary to the proper existence and functioning of persons" (Erickson, 221).

In other words, a person's full delight is to be known for what one is as a person. In a relationship where there is excessive domination or subjugation of one party over the other, love will never flourish. The unspoken mystery of love is that it draws the other into union. Union of this kind means that it lifts the participants into a unity that is powerful and productive. Without equality or nearness, in essence, there will be a powerful battle for control. Who will be like whom? Love is a legitimate need, and many studies have proven the truth of this statement. Is it fair or necessary to apply it to God? If He didn't have his needs met could He be trusted? Think about how dangerous God would be if He weren't complete but was always searching for fulfillment in something or someone. Hypothetically and for the sake of discussion, let's assume that God has need-love. Who is there who could satisfactorily love God? If God is infinite he needs a source of infinite love. Who is equal to God in substance who could satisfy all the demands of love on that level?

A common answer to this question is that man could have become the object of God's love? Many believe that God was lonely before creation. If mankind is the object of God's primary need for love, mankind being a creature, finite and temporal, man would be exhausted in his attempts to satisfy God's infinite need for love. Imagine satisfying a person who has all knowledge and power available to themselves. There is another problem, however, if a man was the object of God's need for love, then before man's creation, God was not love. This would say that God became love when Adam was created. God's dependency on any being outside of Himself would throw God into a codependent relationship, and the differential in power would exhaust both of them. So you begin to see the problem, the object of God's love must have been someone equal in substance, eternal, and a member of God's being to satisfy the demands of personhood, love, and biblical description.

The second person of the Trinity is the only one who could meet such requirements: present with the Father from all eternity, and having His own personhood and equal to God in substance. This makes God free and complete within Himself. As He is, the Trinitarian God is not dependent upon the world for any part of His essential character.

1.5 GOD AS SPIRIT

In human relationships, we define the "other" in terms of their relationship to us. When we point to the person who gave us physical life, we call them "father" or "mother". Father or mother is the term for that relationship. When we have an intimate relationship with another human being, we call them "friends." By comparison, a person we don't know at all is a "stranger". A person we travel with is a "companion". A person who takes care of us is a "caretaker". Consider the following terms: wife, boss, acquaintance, teacher, mentor, servant, daughter, pet, and victim. Each one is a label for the relationship he, she, or it has with us. As we apply this understanding to the Godhead, we see that the relational term between the

Father and Son is familial. The Father calls Jesus "My beloved Son." Jesus calls God "My Father." The relational term is how they relate to each other as Father and Son. The domain of the "son" carries with it the idea of "submission, obedience" and the same "genetic material." However, the relationship between the Father, Son, and the Spirit is not familial. The Spirit is not called another *son, uncle*, or *aunt*. By contrast, the Spirit is called the *breath* of God. The word for Spirit in Latin is *spiritus* it means *the breath* which is akin to *spirare*, "Inspire." Hence, we say the Holy Spirit is the *spiritus (S 4151)*: the Spirit of both the Father and the Son. He is the love that flows between them.

Let's look a little deeper.

Espirit de Corp

Dr. Fuller says that civic organizations, such as a church or military clubs are organizations in which the spirit of the group is characterized by a distinctive atmosphere called *"esprit de corps."* This spirit arises from three main factors that would characterize such an organization:

a) The way its members feel about each other.
b) The degree of commitment they have for each other.
c) The degree of dedication its purposes calls forth.

One of the most famous organizations in the US known for its *esprit de corps* is the Marine Corps. In this organization, we see on a human level what it means to have *esprit de corps*. We know that the Marine slogan *Semper Fidelis* means "always faithful to each other, to the Corp, and to the country it serves." The commitment is so strong that it issues forth a "marine spirit." *Espirit de corps* does several things: (1) sets a high ethical standard for its members (2) brings forth a great degree of commitment and loyalty (3) overcomes the basic alienation of man by making him part of something greater than himself. When you apply this to a city, the lack of it may explain the failure of a city to thrive or attract interesting people to it. If any of these three things are missing the city or organization does not become an interesting place to live or visit. Analyze your city. How do the members feel about one another? Are they committed to each other? Do they all love and identify with its purpose? Do they even have a purpose? With these three things in mind, the organization can thrive and continue to attract new people to its midst.

Observing this on a human level shows us the kind of love relationship that exists eternally between the Father and the Son. It exceeds where human imagination leaves off. Let us analyze those three points in the Godhead: (1) the degree of the love between the Father and the Son; (2) the degree of commitment they have for each other; and (3) the degree of dedication to their purpose. So strong, so true and so substantial is this love between the Father and the Son that there comes forth, or eternally generated, a separate person. Yet their unity remains because they are equal in love, purpose, and power. The "I" of the Godhead incorporates all three members of the Trinity and yet they are still distinct in function. Dr. Fuller states,

> The "spirit" of this community is so strong that a separate center of consciousness called the Holy Spirit proceeds forth both from the Father and the Son in such a way that a third person exists, who Himself is a center of consciousness and has all the divine attributes of the Father and of the Son (Fuller, 123).

The Westminster Confession (1647) states,

> *The Father is of none, neither begotten nor proceeding; the Son is eternally begotten of the Father; the Holy Spirit [is] eternally proceeding from the Father and the Son (Fuller, 121).*

Scripture does not record that the Father loves the Spirit or that the Son loves the Spirit or vice versa. Rather, we read that the Father loves the Son, and the Son loves the Father, and it is the Holy Spirit who sheds this love (the love between the Father and the Son) abroad in our hearts (see Jn. 14:23 and Ro. 5:5). Yet the Spirit is also the perfect expression of God's love. The Holy Spirit is not only the container of the Father's and Son's love, but He is the Love of God. Furthermore, the Spirit is never spoken of as another "son," for to whom else did God say, "You are my Son, today I have begotten You" (Ps. 2:7 and Heb... 1:5 NKVJ). It speaks of the Holy Spirit as one who proceeds from the Father and the Son. Scripture says that both can say the Spirit belongs to each one, "But when the Helper comes, whom I shall send to you...from the Father...the Spirit of Truth, He will testify of Me." Philippians 1:9 names this Spirit as the Spirit of Jesus. Paul exhorts the believers by saying, "For I know that this shall turn out for my deliverance through your prayers and the provision of the Spirit of Jesus Christ." Augustine, the great church scholar, understood the relationship between the persons of the Godhead as:

> *First, there is the One who loves (the Father), and then there is the One who is loved (the Son), and third, there is the Love itself. For this reason and in this understanding, we can say that the Holy Spirit proceeded from both the Father and the Son. (Kelly, 277)*

Considering that the love between the Father and the Son was the consummate and supreme expression of devotion, the fullest expression of love should also proceed forth as a person with all the divine attributes and personality inherent to God. This explains why the Holy Spirit is not just a force or energy that proceeds forth from God, but a Spirit who is also God. Like human love which brings forth children, the presence of children in a relationship demands that the parent share their love with the child. If parents are too young and immature and only have eyes for each other, the child will be emotionally neglected. Perfect love can love in such a way that it is not only receiving but giving. In the Godhead, the addition of a third person ensures that no corruption of the divine love can occur.

Discussion Questions

1. Explain briefly how it is that the attribute of love involves more than one person. If Christ were not the object of God's love, could mankind have suited his purposes for this?

2. How does the concept of self and other work out in your life? Who defined your "self" as an infant? Grade School and High School? Does it remain the same throughout your life? Can it change? How does God fit into your idea of self and others?

3. How does the Holy Spirit generate from the Father and the Son? What is the nature of His relationship to the other two members of the Trinity?

4. The unity of the Godhead hinges on the word *"Echad"*. How would you explain this word in its fullest meaning to a Jew?

5. In Exodus 3:15 God states that His eternal name is "I AM." A name is a marker of who or what a person is. So what and who is He? Why does he refer to eternity in this verse? What is eternity?

Bibliography

Carr, Adrian. *The Separation Thesis of Self and Other Meta theorizing a Dialectal Alternative*, University of Western Sydney. Calvary Theological Seminary, A.carr@uws.edu.au

Erickson, Millard. *God in Three Persons, A Contemporary Interpretation of the Trinity.* Grand Rapids, MI: Baker Book House, 1995.

Fuller, Daniel. *Unity of the Bible.* Grand Rapids, MI: Zondervan Publishing House, 1992.

Hodge, Charles. *Systematic Theology.* New York, New York: Charles Scriber's Sons, 1891.

Kelly, J.N.D. *Early Christian Doctrines,* New York, New York, Harper Collins Press, 1988. Second Printing.

McGill, N. and Ian P. McGreal, *Masterpieces of Christian Literature in Summary Form.* New York, N.Y.: Harper and Row, 1963.

Chapter Two

THE MYSTERY OF ETERNITY

The man was closing the doors of the Empire State Building's deck at midnight. Pushing an old wide wooden broom, he rested against the railing. He took in a deep breath and relaxed, happy to be living in a metropolis that teemed with excitement. At the very same moment that he rested, the grid governing the Manhattan lights shut down, plunging the city into what seemed like outer darkness. He could see nothing. Rubbing his eyes as if to clear away the film, he grew alarmed that it wasn't his eyes, but that something had happened to the city. Everything was dark. He didn't trust himself to even get to the stairwell, so dark was the night. As he crawled around the edge of the wall, he continued to blink involuntarily, unconvinced that the darkness was real. His natural eyes strained to see something, anything, but all that could be detected was the heavy dull sound of nothing. As he stared with the opaque eyes of a blind man, he could almost the waves of darkness crashing into each other. Were his eyes playing games with him? It seemed to him there were oceans of darkness all around him. (Author Unknown)

2.1 GOD OF THE DARKNESS

We begin by imagining a time and place in which nothing yet existed, no sun, stars, or even earth. There was not even the presence of light; all that existed was immense darkness that in its totality is unimaginable. This is where our story begins—in complete darkness. In our search, we turn to Ps. 18:11 which says, *"He made <u>darkness</u> His secret place his pavilion round about him were dark waters and thick clouds of the skies."* KJV

The term "pavilion of darkness" is a double metaphor which means that each one stands on its own and that neither one sheds light on the other. Each metaphor must be looked at independently to understand the spiritual meaning. The term "darkness" *(Chosek-S2822)* is a term of secrecy or hiddenness." It refers to obscurity, or better yet, a secret place. *Chosek* is used in Gen. 1:2ff where it says, "darkness" *(chosek)* was on the face of the deep." The NLT Psalm 18:11 says it like this, "He shrouded himself in darkness *(Cheshkah S2824)* veiling his approach with dark rain clouds." The NASB says it like this, "He made darkness *(Cheshkah S2824)* His hiding place, His canopy round about Him, darkness *(Araphel S6205)* of waters, thick clouds of the skies." Remember that grandeur is often described in oceanic terms in the Bible. It's a symbolic way of describing something vast, for example, the immensity of our oceans directly points to the magnitude of God. This imagery paints a profound picture of the great cosmic seas that God lives in that the Bible calls "waters." In the natural realm, the enormity of deep space points to the greatness of these pavilions which not only surround Him but also obscure Him for the term "darkness" (*Chosek S 2821*) is a term of secrecy or hiddenness.

The term "pavilion" (*sukkah S 5521*) describes a stage or an open-air shelter of an elaborate nature. To grasp the height and depth of God's word, the Bible speaks to us in architectural terms, i.e., "Pavilions". These terms speak to us of enormous pillars and curtains, that tells us this backdrop is for the drama which is about to take place. Since this is a divine backdrop, the "tent" takes on a more religious connotation: the idea of a heavenly cathedral, in which "clouds, stars, and suns" are to play a majestic role in the future life of man as a religious entity. This idea is captured beautifully in the word "dome" or vault of heaven.

2.2 GOD AS MISCHAN

Pavilion or residence is encapsulated in the Hebrew word *Mishkan (S 4908),* or tabernacle which carries the idea of a tent of residence. Job 36:29 reads, "Can anyone understand the spreadings of the clouds or the noise of his tabernacle?" The English word "tabernacle" is derived from the Latin *Tabernaculum* meaning "tent" or "hut." In ancient Roman history, this was a ritual structure. "Sanctuary" is also used for the biblical tabernacle as well as the phrase "tent of meeting." The Hebrew word *Mishkan (S 4908)* implies "dwelling," or a "place of rest.'

Shekinah is based on the Hebrew root word *Mishkan (S 4908)*: a glory presence that dwelt within this divinely ordained structure, a euphemism for God's Presence. Ps.18 as well as other verses tell us that this "pavilion" is where the presence of God dwells. He is our Dwelling Place, our Tent. This would be consistent with Ps. 90:1 which says, "You have been our dwelling place *(Mishkan* or *Tabernacle)* in all generations." It is not a stretch to say that all of reality has its reality in God or that God is our Tent. This could have been what Paul had in mind when he said, "...He is not far from each one of us; for in Him we live and move and have our being..." (Acts 17: 28).

The everlasting Presence of God is a tabernacle for the whole created realm. As to the clouds that surround Him in Ps. 18:11 we are to think shade or rest. We are to think of it as a "covering" or a shade for the earth, a symbol of rest and shade for the whole earth. Now what is interesting is that the tabernacle that Moses built was called the Tent of Meeting and is a duplicate of this heavenly reality.

The parallels are striking. Once the tabernacle was consecrated to God, it was filled with the Glorious Presence of the LORD, "Then the cloud covered the Tent of Meeting, and the glory of the LORD filled the tabernacle" (Exodus 40:34). When the temple was completed, "...Fire came down from heaven and consumed the burnt offering and the sacrifices, and the glory of the LORD filled the temple" (2 Ch. 7:1). The Lord Jesus as the fulfillment of the temple was baptized with the Holy Spirit (John 1:32). On the day of Pentecost, "All of them were filled with the Holy Spirit ...." (Acts 2:4.) No longer does God indwell the physical building of stones; now he dwells in the hearts of his people, the "living stones that are being built into a spiritual house" (1 Peter 2:5).

In these texts, God is saying that His divine providence (covering or canopy) will be over all reality: both the natural and the supernatural are indelibly stamped with His Trinitarian image. Professor Bavinck's organic model of the universe is helpful here. His view of the cosmos is patterned after the Trinity. James Eglington in *Trinity and Organism*, says of Bavinck's model,

> "A worldview founded on the Trinitarian doctrine of God must move towards a non-mechanical interpretation of the universe" (67).

Secularism moves us to an impersonal view of life, as a method to interpret our existence. Don't be fooled, science in the hands of godless men and women will always lead us away from God.

Dr. Eglinton continues,

> "What the idea of Trinity does for us ultimately, is to describe a living dynamic where unity and diversity can become a 'superlative kind of unity. The foundation for both diversity and unity is in God... Here is a unity that does not destroy but rather maintains diversity and di-

versity that does not come at the expense of unity, but rather unfolds it in its riches" (67).

The United States is an example of this kind of superlative unity. We are many, both individually and ethnically, yet we are bound by the American ideals of life, which are based upon the Judeo-Christian worldview. As we drift from this to a more mechanical view of life, we separate and become dysfunctional. The Judeo-Christian worldview teaches the reality of sin and evil, the 10 commandments, to forgive, to face responsibility, if a man doesn't work, he doesn't eat, and many more. Other nations cannot begin to compare to the US without upholding these values. Eglinton says,

> First, the created order is marked by simultaneous unity and diversity. This is essential if God is Triune. As the universe itself is a general revelation of God, it must reflect his identity as three in one. Reality, therefore, becomes somewhat triniform: life is a unity of different parts. 'The Christian mind remains unsatisfied until all of existence is referred to the Triune God, and until the confession of God's Trinity functions at the center of our thought and life (67).

2.3 THE TEMPLE IN PLURALITY

Moses was given explicit instructions that reflected a threefold blueprint of the cosmic realities: the outer court, the holy place, and the holy of holies. These reflect a triadic pattern that begins with the Father, the originator and beginning of all activity, the Son who proceeds from the Father as wisdom, and the Spirit who proceeds from both the Father and the Son with the power to complete the consummation of their will in creation, redemption, and glorification.

After the Lord Jesus died and rose again from the dead, He ascended into heaven, from where He sent the Holy Spirit to indwell His people. The Holy Spirit unites believers to the Lord Jesus Christ in all his offices as prophet, priest, and king. In the same way that God in-dwelt the tabernacle and the temple, He now indwells the people of God.

2.4 MAN IN PLURALITY

Man's thought life or consciousness is commonly experienced as a threesome. There is the one who speaks, the one who listens, and the one who decides. This is often referred to as "me, myself, and I" or the id, ego, superego, reason, will, and emotions. Man is also plural in his social life as in the primary family unit of husband, wife, and children in which the divine image is perpetuated. Earth may have been the created realm that gave materiality to the spiritual realm in every facet of its construction. In the current structures, we recognize facets of creation installed to lead fallen man back to Himself and to teach him or her about the unseen dimension of reality.

In summation, man's creation story is set in unbelievable majesty and wonder—a tabernacle of holiness (whole, health) that is most suitable for the beauty of God's love toward man. A spectacular setting for a love affair between Himself and the family of human beings He will soon create and endow with everlasting life. It is a stage that will ultimately display the greatest act of love in human history—the giving of His only Son. The pavilions of darkness speak to a vast theater of drama where the depth of God's wisdom and glory will be both incarnated and displayed in all its grandeur and beauty, reflective of the Artist who gave it life and in part, all of His attributes.

Discussion Questions

1. Why does the author of Scripture use "architectural terms" to describe spiritual reality? Discuss the picture words "pavilions," "waters" and "darkness." What do they communicate?

2. What is God's main purpose in setting the stage? What does it reveal about God?

3. How does the "*mishkan*" point to the idea of a perpetual tabernacle?

4. How is the trinitarian attribute of God manifested in this duplication on earth? Why is this relevant for us?

5. How is the idea of "clouds" and "canopies" similar? What is their spiritual import?

Bibliography

James Eglinton, *Trinity, and Organism*, T&T Clark International 80 Maiden Lane Suite 704 New York, NY 10038, 2012.

Chapter Three

THE MYSTERY OF ANGELS

God moved out of His three-fold glory with a spectacular edict, "Let there be light" the glory of His splendor was about to be seen. His first creation was to build Himself a throne, a kingdom, and suitable inhabitants. Not an earthly creation but a spiritual reality in which he would be worshiped and honored. He was to be worshipped by a host of beings known as angels. Who and what are these beings? How are they different from the heirs of salvation? What is the scope and nature of their being? What was and is their relationship to Adam and Eve? We already have a myriad of questions about angels and their interaction with our own lives.

3.1 ANGELS AS SPIRITS

Commonly understood, as taught by St. Augustine, who says of angels, "'Angel' is the name of their office, not of their nature. If you seek the name of their nature, it is 'spirit,' if you seek the name of their office it is 'angel': from what they are 'spirit,' from what they do, 'angel'" (Augustine, PL 37,1348,188). The Bible says, "Are they not all ministering spirits, sent forth to minister, for them that shall be heirs of salvation?" (Heb.1:14, KJV) As purely spiritual creatures, angels have intelligence and will, they are personal and immortal. Since their fall, however, the fallen angels are in a fixed state of perdition, the obedient angels in a fixed state of glory. They were once all glorious creatures and the splendor with which they were made gives witness to this reality. The Scriptures nowhere attribute to these beings bodies or materiality of any kind. They are invisible and incorporeal. Professor Hodge says, "Their relation to space is described as an *illocalitas* [without locality]; not ubiquity nor omnipresent as they are always somewhere and not everywhere at any given moment" (Hodge,1:636). They are not confined to space but can move freely from one portion of space to another. For a clearer understanding of their movement, we must understand how the human body moves. "Movement," is the sign of life. The soul is the animating spirit of life, hence it is the spirit or soul of a man which determines where or when a man will move. It is not the body that moves, but the soul or the spirit of a man that moves him. James 2:26 says, "...The body without the spirit is dead..."(KJV). This principle applies to angels who are sole "spirits" and can thus move at will without the encumbrance (limitation) of a material body.

As humans, we decide to move, then lift our bodies to accomplish that which we will. For instance, if we decide to take a trip to Europe, it would necessitate packing (clothes to dress us), getting to the airport (a car to transport us), boarding a plane (a vehicle to transport our bodies over the ocean), meals on board (to feed us) and then after 12 to 15 hours would we finally arrive at our desired destination. The amount of energy needed to accomplish this one simple task is enormous. Spirits or angels, however, do not have the encumbrance of bodies and can move as God wills. They do not have to transport "bodies" anywhere. They are free to travel as they desire. God tells them to go and they are there. Just like our souls by taking daily thoughts can pass from one place to another without going through the middle, so can angels thus move from one place to another. For example, imagine yourself at Niagara Falls, experiencing the misty air around your body and the smell of the fresh cool air. How long did it take you to get "there"? The same is true for the movement of angels, i.e., as quick as a thought or the spoken command of God.

Likewise, angels have the power to communicate one with another without the benefit of "ears" and "symbols." They can speak directly, i.e., in a universal language to our spirits (souls) and God. The minute they hear our voice (our thoughts which is the voice of the human spirit), and by God's approval, they are with us. Nu. 20:16 shows this principle, "...When we cried out to the LORD, He heard our voice and sent an angel and brought us out from Egypt," and Is. 30:19, "...at the sound of your cry; when He hears it, He will answer you" (NKJV).

Human spirits, however, must use the medium of sound and the delicate instruments of the ear as well as the intricate symbols of meaning. Over large distances, we must use telephones or letters or email, but angels are not encumbered nor limited by matter, time or space. Unlike humans, which must accumulate knowledge through the senses, angels acquire knowledge directly. For this reason, we attribute to their perfection in their being, that, unlike humans, there is no room for "personal interpretation" or misunderstandings from the world of the senses, which can be distorted. Though angels do not need to assume bodies to live or acquire knowledge for themselves (for their power is greater than bodily power) they often do assume bodies to manifest themselves to human beings (Gen. 18:21; Gen. 19:15) who are limited by materiality.

The principle of "materiality" is not a difficult issue once the basic laws of physics are understood. At the command of God, the energy came forth from his mouth dividing at various speeds. Those things closest to the Infinite Mouth of Life are those things that are invisible and can do "wonders" since they are not bound by time and space. Those things at a lower energy (or heat) at some point take on pure spirit while at even lower levels they materialize into the world that we know and recognize today. A simple example of this is water that has been heated to a certain level turning into gas, and at higher levels into vapors, and so on. The lower the speed of energy (heat) the great the materialization. So angels at some point could materialize if they entered a certain molecular level which requires lower amounts of wattage, or heat. A biblical example of this de-materialization might be in Acts 8:38-40 in which an angel appeared to Philip telling him which direction to find someone ready to receive Christ.

Then this odd occurrence:

> **38** *"And he [Philip] ordered the chariot to stop; and they both went down into the water, Philip as well as the eunuch, and he baptized him.* **39** *When they came up out of the water, the Spirit of the Lord snatched Philip away; and the eunuch no longer saw him, but went on his way rejoicing.* **40** *But Philip found himself at Azotus, and as he passed through he kept preaching the gospel to all the cities until he came to Caesarea."*

Perhaps this "lower-order" of man is what Paul meant when he said that man was made a "little lower than the angels" at least for this present age (Hebrews 2:7 and Ps. 85:5). The text in Luke 20:34-36 speaks of a transfiguration of man when they can no longer die. This text points to the resurrection body that we will have in the hereafter at which point we will be equal to the angels. "Neither can they die anymore: for *they are equal unto the angels*; and are the children of God, being the children of the resurrection" (Luke 20:34-36). Angels at higher speeds, as the need arises, can produce effects in the natural world as unseen and invisible beings. This has serious implications in the natural world (Job 1:6,7; 2:6) for among their effects can come apparitions, visions, voices, inspirations, and even doctrines (1 John 4:1). They can, for example, produce effects in the minds of men (Gen. 3:1-7; Job 4:15; 1 Tim. 4:1). Examples of this can be seen all through history, as in the angel that appeared to Mohammed, and Joseph Smith, or even the apparitions of the Virgin and her "image" in places all around the world. For this reason, John exhorts us to "test the spirits" to see if they are from God. "Spirits" can mean apparitions of angels, or spirit beings (1 Tim 3:1-5)

3.2 A CREATED HOST

Ps. 33:6 says, "By the word of the Lord, the heavens were made, and all the host of them by the breath of His mouth" which strongly suggests that angels were created simultaneously, that is, they constituted a "created host," in distinction from a race which propagates one at a time. Angels do not have a separate existence, a different agenda from God's, but were created to carry out various functions in God's economy.

Within the "created host" however, there is evidence of order and diversity. Col. 1:16 tells us that He made them in organized categories of thrones, dominions, principalities, and powers. According to Ephesians 6, these orders exist in the heavenly realm to this day. Diversity can also be seen in the various names of angels, such as the cherubim, the seraphim, as well as angels, and archangels. We ask, What is their role and how do they affect the natural world in which we live? Let us begin to look at the helpful tool shown in Gen. 28:11-12:

> *"And so he [Jacob] came to a certain place and stayed there all night because the sun had set. And he took one of the stones of that place and put it at his head, and he lay down in that place to sleep. Then he dreamed, and be-*

hold, a ladder was set up on the earth, and its top reached to heaven, and there the angels of God were ascending and descending on it. And behold the Lord stood above it and said, "I am the LORD God of Abraham your father and the God of Isaac..."

Angels (Angelos)

Using the helpful tool of Jacob's ladder, we will ascend the scale to get a better view of the landscape of heaven. Placing our feet upon the first rung of the ladder, no doubt the first kind of angel we would see are the angels which are entrusted with the care of believers, i.e., "The heirs of salvation." We say this because Genesis 28:12 says that these angels are always "ascending and descending," they "ascend" to the Father, rather than descend revealing that their primary location is on earth (where believers dwell) and from the earth, they ascend to the Father. These are the angels to which Jesus refers as "the angels that always see the Father's face." Matthew 18:10 records the words of Jesus saying, "Take heed that you do not despise one of these little ones, for I say unto you, that in heaven, their angels always see the face of My Father who is heaven." (NKJV) The phrase "little ones," contrary to popular belief, does not refer to "little children" but to the disciples of Jesus who are God's little ones, i.e., His children, i.e., the heirs of salvation. These angels are responsible for aiding and saving the lives of men as God dictates. For instance, the power of God in saving a drowning man in a vast ocean would be the work of an angel. In the same way, God sends angels (unaware by men) to bring messages and warnings to save lives. God can speak directly to man or he can also use these messengers at His will.

Archangels (angelos, arche)

As we ascend the ladder, we would then see the archangels. These are the angels who know divine mysteries, and who are sent on important and serious occasions. Of these, we read that the great Archangel Gabriel was sent to Daniel,

> *"...While I was still speaking in prayer, then the man Gabriel, whom I had seen in the vision previously, came to me in my extreme weariness about the time of the evening offering" (Daniel 9:21).*

Then Gabriel appeared to Mary, to announce the coming Deliverer (Luke 1:26). The term "archangel" is generally taken to mean "chief, leading or foremost" angel (Jude 9; 1 Thess. 4:16). They generally have a critical role in salvation history (Jn. 5:4 and Rev. 12:7-9) as in the Annunciation and the Apocalypse of Revelation. It was the Archangel Michael (meaning "Who is like God?") who fought with the dragon and overcame the Devil and his angels. Through his victory, a third of the angels who rebelled against God were cast out of heaven (Rev 12:7). The Bible predicts another such conflict at the end of the age. This time, however, he (Satan) will be "cast out" of the earth, as it were, in one great and mighty exorcism (Rev 18:10; 20:10). Gabriel (meaning "The power of God") was not only present at the birth of Jesus but most likely also the angel who attended Jesus in the Garden of Gethsemane. Might we conclude that Jesus' angel was Gabriel Himself, having been with Jesus since His birth?

The Powers (Dunamis)

Going higher on "Jacob's ladder," we would come upon what is termed "the powers" *(Dunamis)*. These "powers" perform signs and wonders in and through the elements on the earth or near earth itself. They often instruct and warn men. For example, the signs and wonders performed in Dt. 6:22 "and the Lord showed signs and wonders, before our eyes, great and severe against Egypt, Pharaoh, and all his household" were performed at the command of God, *(Jehovah, Yahweh)* through the good angels who are called the "powers" (Col. 1:15-17).

Wherever work needs to be performed in the material world, you will see the work of the "powers," which are God's ambassadors to do His will. This work in the material world ranges from small acts of protection to moving hoards of locusts into the land to devour the grains of Egypt as seen in the Exodus plagues. Though they are still personal spirits, nowhere are we given to understand or know their names. They were discreetly behind the scenes, unlike Gabriel and Michael.

A fascinating study of the word "winds" serves to indicate how the "powers" operate and their range of power and authority over the material world as God allows. In the Exodus story, the text says, "So Moses stretched out his rod over the land of Egypt, and the LORD brought an east wind on the land all that day..." (Ex.10:13). Etymologically, the word "wind" is the same as "Ruach" which is the word for "spirit" or "spirits." The word for "wind" in this verse is *"Ruach"* which is the same word used for the *Ruach* of a man or the "spirit of a man" which is to say it is or refers to a personal living being.

Thus we take it to mean that the winds spoken of in these references are really "spirits" or as we know them, angels who in their nature are spirits. God Himself is called *"Ruach Elohim"* or the "wind of God." Thus the word *"Ruach"* or "Spirit" as used in Exodus 10:13, (see above) can be seen as *"ruach"* as personal living beings who brought in the locusts.

Verse 19 of the same chapter reads, "And the LORD turned a very strong west wind, which took the locusts away and blew them into the Red Sea." Genesis 14:21 says, "...And the LORD caused the sea to go back by a strong east wind all that night, and made the sea into dry land, and the waters were divided." Verse 15:10 says, "You blew with Your wind, the sea covered them; they sank like lead in the mighty waters." Thus, we say that the good angels are the powers of God through the work of the "winds" as seen throughout Scripture. In support of this idea, Professor Kittel says the following,

> *It is no accident that the same Hebrew word "Ruach" is used for both "spirit" and "wind." The wind is very powerful; it is indeed irresistible in its force. It also is mysterious,*

"The wind bloweth where it listeth, and thou hearest the sound thereof, but canst tell whence it cometh, and whither it goeth (Jn.3:8). Mysterious and unfathomable forces are at one in this with the wind. Those divine forces are breathing, a "Ruach," of God. They are known as divine powers which bring either deliverance or destruction (Kittle, 7:367).

The divine powers are associated with the activity of the weather, wind, storms, and lightning and are spoken of as the actions of God. Genesis 8:1 says, "Then God remembered Noah, and every living thing, and all the animals that were with him in the ark. And God made a wind (*Ruach, spirit, angel*) to pass over the earth, and the waters subsided" (NKJV). Genesis 41:27 says that an east wind (*Ruach, spirit, angel*) caused the famine which forced Jacob and his family to travel to Egypt, while Exodus 19:16 says, "Then it came to pass on the third day, in the morning, that there were thunderings and flashes of lightning, and a thick cloud on the mountain; and the sound of the trumpet was very loud..." (NKJV). Dt. 33:2 tells us that those "thunders and flashes of lightning" were the myriad of angels that accompanied the LORD. (Also see Numbers 11:31; Ps. 18:10; 104:3, 4; 107:25; 147:18; 148:8; Ez 1:4ff; Mt 24:31; John 3:8; Acts 2:2; Revelation 7:1-3; 8:5,7; Dan 7:10; Acts 7:53;) A truly biblical worldview does not attribute changes in the weather to impersonal (so-called natural causes of "mother nature") natural forces or processes, rather are the unseen hands of angels—both good and evil angels in the fallen world.

These powers are also associated with astronomical phenomena throughout the Bible. For instance, in the book of Judges, we see this evidenced clearly in Chapter 5:20. The scene is one of a battle on the earth between Israel (Deborah) and the Canaanite Lord Sisera. But verse 20 shows the spiritual and heavenly battle occurring simultaneously "They [the angels] fought from the heavens; the stars from their courses fought against Sisera." (NKJV) Matt. 24:29 (NKJV) says, "Immediately after the tribulation of those days the sun will be darkened, and the moon will not give its light; the stars will fall from heaven, and the powers of the heavens will be shaken" indicating a close coupling of the two spheres—the natural (the stars) and the supernatural powers (Also see Jude 13, Revelation 1:20; 8:10-12; 12:4.)For this reason when we read in the Gospel "There will be signs in the sun, in the moon and the stars" (Luke 21:25 KJV) and then "...for the powers of heaven will be shaken," (Luke 21:26 KJV), we must consider these to be the spirits (angels) through whom powerful signs take place (Ps. 135:9).

Powers can refer to both the good powers of the Lord or to evil powers that dwell in the "air." The good powers check the powers of darkness as shown in Zech.... 1:11 when the angels say, "We have walked to and fro throughout the earth, and behold, all the earth is resting quietly." These "powers" bind the evil of this world, so that it can do no evil, nor any harm when appropriated by believers through prayer. When Jesus says the following in Luke 22:53 "When I was daily with you in the temple, ye stretched forth no hands against me; but this is your hour, and the power of darkness" (KJV). This "power of darkness" is a personal power that Jesus is referring to, not just a neutral power or a natural force, but an evil malevolent being that seeks to undo and destroy. Within this framework, when Jesus rebuked the "winds" in Matthew 8:24-27, that spoke to a demonic angel who had charge of the weather and had been harassing the disciples in reaching the shore on the other side of the lake. John Calvin's perspective is helpful at this point:

> *God controls the government of the universe. No wind ever arises or increases except by God's express command. Further, since angels are the powers of God, it follows that they never cease from their office of working. For God never can rest; he sustains the world by his energy, he governs everything however minute, so that not even a sparrow falls to the ground without his decree.*

Martin Luther went further than Calvin by saying that the Psalmist's view of the wind as having wings is true in the truest sense of the word. He said,

> "The devil provokes such storms, but good winds are produced by good angels. Winds are nothing but spirits, either good or evil. The devil sits there and snorts, and so do the angels when the winds are salubrious" (Luther).

Finally, in the book of Revelation, we are told of four angels who have charge over the "four winds that blow from the four corners of the earth" (Rev 7:1).

Principalities (principados, arche)

> Beyond the "powers" are the "princes" or "principalities" "by whose moderation and wisdom every power on earth is set up, ruled, kept within bounds, transferred, diminished, altered" (Evans, 153). (See also Romans 8:38; 1 Cor. 15:24; Eph.... 1:21; 6:10; Col 1:16; 2:10;15.)

Principalities are those celestial beings whose function is to govern large territories of land. There is a reference to two such principalities (evil ones) in Daniel 10:20, the "Prince of Persia" and the "Prince of Greece." That this perspective is within the margins of classical Christianity is shown in the works of F. F. Bruce, a well-known evangelical scholar and author, who says this is indeed what Dt. 32:8 means, "When the Most High gave to the nations their inheritance, When he separated the children of men, He set the bounds of the peoples, according to the number of the angels of God."

Principalities are also addressed in the Revelation of John when Jesus refers to the seven churches and their angels--to their messengers. These are good angels *(arche)* in charge of the churches throughout the ages. They are the angels of Ephesus (Rev. 2:1), Smyrna (Rev. 2:8), Pergamum (Rev 2:12). Thyatira (Rev 2:18), Sardis (Rev. 3:1), Philadelphia (Rev. 3:7),

Laodicea (Rev. 3:14).

Dominions (kuriotes/kratos)

Above the principalities, as we move up the ladder, we would come to the realm of the "dominions" who are angels ranked higher still. Their work is of a very high level, for they are the masters (rulers) of the principalities and guardians of the powers, determining and releasing the work of the "virtues" in the heavens, and providing care and provision for the angels' work on earth.

The Virtues (might): They are sometimes referred to as "the shining ones." They are responsible for acts of courage, grace, and valor assisting the Holy Spirit in His work toward the saints. Wikipedia says, "The 'Virtues' or 'Strongholds' lie beyond the *ophanim* [Thrones/Wheels]. Their primary duty is to supervise the movements of the heavenly bodies to ensure that the cosmos remains in order. The term appears to be linked to the attribute "might" from the Greek root δύναμις in Ephesians 1:21 which is also translated as "virtue." They have presented as the celestial Choir "Virtues," in *the Summa Theologica*. Traditional theological conceptions of the Virtues might appear to describe the same Order called the Thrones [Gr. T*hronos*].

> "The name of the holy Virtues signifies a certain powerful and unshakable virility welling forth into all their Godlike energies; not being weak and feeble for any reception of the divine Illuminations granted to it; mount-

ing upwards in the fullness of power to an assimilation with God; never falling away from the Divine Life through its weakness, but ascending unwaveringly to the super-essential Virtue which is the Source of virtue: fashioning itself, as far as it may, in virtue; perfectly turned towards the Source of virtue, and flowing forth providentially to those below it, abundantly filling them with virtue" (Pseudo-Dionysius).

Perhaps it is a significant point when Jesus was touched by the woman with the issue of blood, that He said, "Who touched Me? ...Someone touched me; I know that power (virtue) has gone out from me." (Luke 8:46) See also Luke 5:17 in which it is said, "...That the power (virtue) of the Lord was present for him to heal the sick."

Thrones (thronos)
Above the dominions, and higher still are the "thrones," which reach to the Heavenly City itself. These are called "thrones" because they are seated and God is seated with them. To be "seated" with God means literally to bathe in the sea of tranquility that God Himself rests on and is indeed the "peace which surpasses all understanding." Hence, the Lord *of Sabbath* has placed "thrones" around Himself. They are said to be angels of pure humility and submission.

The Cherubim (kerubim)
Immediately above the thrones are the "cherubim" (meaning "to be near" or "held fast") who drink from the very fount of

wisdom, the mouth of God. 1 Kings 6:23 shows us their proximity to the throne of God, "Inside the inner sanctuary, he made two cherubim of olive wood...." As a result of their nearness to God, they can pour forth wisdom from the mouth of God, heavenly wisdom, which Ps. 46:5 says, "...Is [that] river, whose streams, shall make glad the City of God." The *cherubim* (plural of cherub) are full of wisdom for it is said of them that they are to be in the "fullness of knowledge," for the Lord is a God of knowledge (1 Sam. 2:3) for in Him there is no darkness at all, no ignorance of any kind (Evans, 153).

From this angelic hierarchy so far we can see that the cherubim are the second-highest angels in rank. They have an intimate knowledge of God and continually praise Him and are even called in the Scriptures, the *Cherubim*s of glory (2 Kings 19:15; Hebrews 9:5). *The Seraphim (seraphim)*

Above the Cherubim are the Seraphim, (meaning "fiery") who are aflame with the divine fire of God, who kindle the residents of Heaven perpetually, "so that each citizen of Heaven is a burning and shining light, burning with love, shining with knowledge" (Evans, 154). However, the fire which burns with love can also be seen as the fire that burns for judgment and wrath. The seven angels of Revelation 8 are likely of the Seraphim order. These angels stand before God and are given seven trumpets. They also come with burning coals of judgment, signifying their fiery nature (see Is. 6:5). The first angel was given the incense cups which held the prayers of the saints which were then mixed with fire from the altar of God and hurled to the ground as fiery judgments. "...and there were noises, thunderings, flashes of lightning and an earthquake" (Rev. 8:5). The procession of a judgment of fire and destruction indicates the work of the Seraphim. Rev. 8:10 says, "...And a great star fell from heaven, burning like a torch, and it fell on a third of the rivers, and the springs of the waters." It continues with dread and woe saying, "Woe, woe, woe to the inhabitants of the earth, because of the remaining blasts of the trumpet of the three angels who are about to sound" (Rev. 8:13).

3.3 THE PURPOSE OF ANGELS

The description of the angel world reveals attributes of God Himself. Just as men are given spiritual gifts, (wisdom, exhortation, foreknowledge, deliverance, etc.), to glorify the Lord in their character and gifting, so too does the angelic world receive gifts of the omniscience, power, and majesty of God. The cherubim reflect His wisdom. The seraphim reflect His burning passionate love and yet also shows God's wrath for those who hate love. In the Dominions and Principalities, we see his might and order. In the powers, we see His complete control over all the created realm. In the archangels, we see His plans to involve man in everything He wants to do, and in the angels, we see His incredible benevolent love for those who love Him. (See Isaiah 6:1-5.)

The creation of the angelic world was the first thing God created, the inauguration of God's kingdom in heaven. Angels were to serve as God's royal subjects, they were designed to know God, be in His presence, and glorify Him in word and deed. God had endowed (gifted) them with the necessary means to fill His courts with glory, praise, and wonder. Even the celestial creatures that run *to and fro* as lightning (Ezek. 1:13,14) were designed to demonstrate God's immense greatness. The angelic world was created to demonstrate the highest royal court in all of reality. God was to be the Great King, the King of Kings, and the Lord of Hosts.

Furthermore, the angels were to attend the presence of God, as couriers, as subjects of His heavenly kingdom, as well as serve as His standing army. Dt. 33:2 says of the giving of the Law on Mt. Sinai, "The Lord came from Sinai...He came with ten thousand saints....(holy ones)." Ps. 68:17 tells us that these holy ones were angels, "The chariots of God are twenty thousand, even thousands of thousands; the Lord is among them, as in Sinai, in the Holy Place" (See also Acts 7:53). Ezekiel 1:24 indicates the awesome power of these spirit creatures and the majesty with which they surround the throne of God saying, "When they went, I heard the noise of their wings, the noise of many waters...a tumult like the noise of an army."

The biblical view of the universe is throbbing with life and pervades all levels of reality. The cosmos is heavily populated with "legions" and "myriads" of angelic beings, of various ranks and species, and not the empty space it looks like from the "naked" and undiscerning eye.

Since we see that the spirit world is filled with a multitude of angels, which the Bible calls "myriads" it behooves us to ask, "Why? Why would this be so?" When we read the first chapter of Genesis, we hear God say, "Let the world teem with life!" and, "Let it bring forth abundantly!" God wanted to fill the earth with life, which according to Genesis 1 was "very good." He could just as well have said, "My creation is perfect!" This reflects my glory! Hence multitudes, or millions of species of all kinds of life, trees, plants, animals, and insects, speak about God's perfection and His glory. God's glory is seen in the multitude, in the excellence of quality but also vast quantity. Astronomers often speak of the beauty of space, of its perfection, mathematically and cosmically, which reveals to the student of the Bible and the pursuer of God, the majesty and unlimited power of God.

Discussion Questions

1. Professor Hodge says of angels, "Their relation to space is described as an *illocalitas* [without locality]; not ubiquity nor omnipresent as they are always somewhere and not everywhere at any given moment" (Hodge,1:636). Compare and contrast how men's movements are different from angels.

2. This course speculates that man was made a little lower than the angels at least for this present age. This refers to what part of man? "Yet you made them only a little lower than the angels and crowned them with glory and honor." (Hebrews 2:7 and Ps. 85:5)

3. The evidence of order and diversity in Col. 1:16 tells us that He made angels in organized categories of thrones, dominions, principalities, and powers to demonstrate what about God?

4. The "powers" work through signs and wonders in and through the elements on the earth or near earth itself. Can you give biblical evidence of such an event?

5. The biblical view of the universe is throbbing with life, pervading all levels of reality. The cosmos is heavily populated with "legions" and "myriads" of angelic beings, of various ranks and species, and not the empty space it looks like from the "naked" and undiscerning eye. Where do the fallen angels dwell in your opinion?

Bibliography

Aquinas, Thomas, *The Summa Theologica,* Five Volumes, (Christian Classic, 1981)

Augustine, En Ps. 103:1-15; PL 37,1348,188

Calvin, John, *Institutes of Christian Religion*, London England: Westminster: John Knox Press, 1559 Translation edition, June 1960.

Hodge, Charles, *Systematic Theology*. Charles Scribner and Sons 1891, New York, NY, 1891.

Kittle, Gerard, *Theological Dictionary of the New Testament.* Eerdmans Publishing House, Grand Rapids, MI 1967.

Evans, G.R. General Editor, Bernard de Clairvaux, Selected Works, Western Spiritual Classics, Paulist, New York, New York, 1987.

Pseudo-Dionysius the Areopagite's De Coelestia Hierarchia.

Chapter Four

THE MYSTERY OF EVIL

So just as the angels (as well as men for that matter) reveal the various attributes of God, i.e., some reveal His love, some His knowledge, in others His power (1 Cor. 12:7). God also revealed His beauty and wisdom in one specific and a special angel named Lucifer. To understand the creation and subsequent fall we turn to Ezekiel 28 which prophetically describes what happened at the original creation of Lucifer, as an angel of light and his subsequent demise. Although Ez. 28, is talking about the Prince of Tyre, we also understand that the Luciferian spirit operates through worldly thrones and rulers. For this reason, the prophet can speak to both men and to the agent of evil at the same time. An obvious case is Jesus rebuking Satan although physically he was speaking to Peter.

The biblical record seems to say that the greatest of all the created angels was Lucifer. He was given a place of great authority and power over the other angels. We assume this for several reasons: (1) a special mention of his unique creation in Ezekiel 28:13-14 and (2) the special things that were created for him on the day he was created. (3) His anointing is singular, evidence of a special need (4) His threat to extend himself onto the throne of God points to his evident leadership skills.

4.1 THE SEAL OF PERFECTION

Ezekiel 28 gives us an insight into the details of Lucifer's creation and the unsurpassed beauty of his garments. We will look at each section step by step in Ezekiel 28:11-17.

"You were the seal of perfection..."

Ezekiel 28:12 says of him, "You had the seal of perfection..." (NAS). The word perfection in Hebrew *(Khaleel)* means "whole and complete." In other words, Lucifer lacked nothing and "sealed the measure." Another way of saying this is that he was the "total of wisdom and beauty" in the created realm. The word for perfection in Greek, is *"telios"* "coming to the point for which you were created, nothing missing, nothing broken." Lucifer had arrived at the full maturity of his brightness.

Included in the idea of "perfection" is the notion of weight, for the word "perfect" means the full measure, i.e., "heavy." One definition of the word "glory" (Greek *doxa*) refers to "heavy" or that which refers to "weighty substance." Lucifer was indeed glorious, created far above all the other angels. The implication of this is staggering. Theologically speaking to be perfected means that this vessel possessed wisdom, knowledge, and divine stature. This makes the choices Lucifer made doubly difficult to understand from a human perspective. The text goes on to tell us what his perfection consisted of.

"Perfect in beauty..."

The Scriptures say that Lucifer was "perfect in beauty..." Lucifer means "light-bearer" or "bright morning star" and God Himself called him "the son of the morning" (Is 14:12). As we have already seen, the natural world is a reflection of the spiritual world, and as such, we can visualize all the stars and yet how much brighter is the morning star which we know to be the planet, Venus. A simple gaze into the heavens at night, or perhaps in the morning, reveals the tremendous difference between this "morning star" and all the other stars. The beauty of Lucifer was truly great and all the spirits must have paled by comparison. Continuing, we read of Lucifer's great beauty:

> "You were in Eden, the garden of God; every precious stone was your covering, the ruby, topaz, and the diamond, the beryl, the onyx, and the jasper, the *lapis lazuli*, the turquoise, and the emerald; and the gold the workmanship of your settings and sockets, was in you. On the day that you were created they were prepared" (Eke. 28:13 NAS).

"Perfect in wisdom" (S 2451)

Wisdom is greater than knowledge since it includes the ability to discern good from evil. One may know but still not be able to see the "signs of the times" while a wise man can avoid trouble without strain just because he is wise. Lucifer had both, wisdom and knowledge. This tells us that Lucifer's perfection included not only physical grace but moral, intellectual, and spiritual gifts as well. Continuing we read,

> "You were on the holy mountain of God; you walked amid the stones of fire. You were blameless in your ways, from the day you were created" (NIV). This seems to indicate that Lucifer was able to walk upon the fiery flames of God's purity and holiness, what the Bible elsewhere describes as "the sea of glass" (Rev. 4:6; 15:2). A place so holy that its glory was like a devouring flame (Exodus 24:17).

> "You were anointed as a guardian cherub, for so I ordained you..."

The Bible also states that Lucifer was especially "anointed" or set apart from the rest of creation by an unusual and special anointing *"mimshach"* (Ez 28:14). The meaning of this word is "expansion." Lucifer's role as the closest of all cherubim demanded special equipping and therefore to equip him for service. God added to his person an expansion, with far-reaching powers. *Expansion* carries it with the notion of "exaltation." Where we can see the significance is in the idea of God having increased his "wingspan." This idea of "wings" is used in the bible as a symbol of authority and protectorate, often used of God who is "like an eagle that stirs up its nest and hovers over its young, that spreads its wings to catch them and carries them on its pinions (Dt. 32:11). The size of the wingspan is always related to the size of the body (as in a group or congregation) to be carried to heaven in worship or preaching.

It is used only once in the Old Testament, and it is used precisely for Lucifer in Ezekiel 28:14. The root word, *Mashah*, is used 68 times all of which are used for anointing someone or something. *This word usage points to God doing the anointing, not man.* When you look at the Greek translation of *"mimshah"* you discover the word "Chi-Rho" or *Christus* in Latin. The New Testament "anointed one" was always referred to as the Messiah, from which we get from the root word *"mimshah."* Keeping in mind the idea of "wingspan" we see that those who have come under the covenant-keeping God and His Christ also come under His giant wingspan, His colossal protectorate.

The Online Etymology Dictionary c.1300, translates *Messias,* from L.L. *Messias,* from Gk. *Messias,* from Aramaic *meshiha* and Heb... *mashiah* "anointed" (of the Lord), from *mashah* "anoint." This is the word rendered in Septuagint as Gk. *Khristos* (see Christ). Old Testament prophetic writing was used for the expected deliverer of the Jewish nation. The transferred sense of "an expected liberator or savior of a captive people" became the popular meaning of this word. Could Lucifer have thought that He was to be the Messiah the answer to everyone's problems?

Lucifer's official creation was that of a cherub (Hebrew *kerub*). Scriptures say, "You were the anointed cherub who covers." Twice Lucifer is called the "covering cherub." Other biblical references place the golden cherubim (Hebrew *kerubim*) at either end of the mercy seat covering the ark of the covenant. They protected the sacred objects that the ark housed and provided with outstretched wings a pedestal for the invisible throne of God (see Ex 25:18 and Hebrews 9:5). The term "covereth" again points us back to the idea of authority or position over a group of people (Ex. 26:31; 1 Kings 6:26).

Thus the Scriptures can use the term "...the cherub who covereth" as a special term designating his special role and high rank over a large body of people or in this case, "spirits." This understanding would then support the use of a special anointing *"mimshah"* (S 4473) to appoint and equip one in such proximity to the God-head. In Lucifer's case, God had given him far-reaching unparalleled powers, but that was not enough for him. He over-reached his anointing, his powers, and took them into his own hands. His pride caused him to overreach his wing-span by his virtues, his intelligence, his beauty, and subsequently, took a third of the angels down with him.

With this in mind Exodus 30:32 tells us that it is a criminal offense to compound the holy anointing oil for a common purpose and use (Douglas, 39). The holy oil represents a fundamental act of God; it is used to confirm God's presence, His approval, and blessing. It consecrates the vessel's legitimacy before God and His people. It creates awe in the eyes of God's people (Numbers 11:17-29). The anointing appoints someone to a special place or function, and as such is equivalent to and symbolizes the Spirit of God. Anointing today still carries with it the same purpose. Whenever God anoints a vessel He means to convey to His people, what was expressed in Exodus 23:20 "Beware of Him and obey His voice and provoke Him not... for My name is in him..." God intends to put fear (true respect and reverence) in our hearts for those He anoints. Hence it is no small matter to ask for God's anointing! It is no small matter to covet the powers of God without obedience to God as protection (1 Samuel 10:6,10;16:13,14).

We ask, what is the significance of being in such proximity to God? We take our clues from the Old Testament, in which nothing fleshly could even come near the mountain where God made His glory to dwell. (Remember God warned Moses to keep back all the beasts or animals from the base of the mountain in Exodus 25.) Its fullest meaning is that no sinful flesh can draw near to God much less ascend the mountain of God. Hence we must understand that for Lucifer to be so close and cover God means several very significant things.

First, it meant that Lucifer as "the anointed cherub" would have been in a position to directly gaze into the ark of God, i.e., into the heart of the Trinity itself, the center and core of all consoling goodness. Being able to draw that near to God (the source of all created reality) would have brought immense revelation and wisdom. Human perception and language fail to adequately capture what this kind of direct access to God would have meant. Even the most mystical of saints have only seen but a glimmer of God, always seeing His glory through a glass darkly. We get a glimmer of this terrible and awesome thing when we look at the phrase "to walk among the fiery stones." The mystics of the Church often refer to this as the way of wisdom or "the mystical darkness of God's incomprehensibility." Professor Kittel says that it indicated an "elevated sense of being," in the same sense as "walking where only God can walk" (Job 9:8, 38:16), (Kittel, X:942). For Lucifer it would have been revealed and visible. It would have meant that as "the covering cherub," and as a created spiritual anointed being, he would have been able to directly perceive the foreknowledge of God.

What does it mean to see them on this level? The veil on the mysteries of God is only revealed to those who fear His name by the Spirit. Thus gifts of the Spirit are carefully guarded and dispersed to whom only God wills (1 Cor. 12:1-5). Lucifer made to dwell in the inner courts (inside the veil) of the Lord's house came to understand that God planned to "make sons" and have them rule and reign with Him. He understood that his role as "chief angel" would always be submissive to the new race of men.

Lucifer's glimpse into the foreknowledge of God also meant that not only did he see the potential realities of mankind, but to his surprise, he most likely also foresaw his dominion (lordship) over humanity in the matrix of time and space (*Clairvaux*, 129). Sadly, rather than allowing this revelation to acknowledge God's great and majestic character, it became, in the final analysis, the unbearable temptation to pride and dominion. Here begins Lucifer's choice, like Adam, his confirmation to follow God or to follow what he had seen in the foreknowledge of God.

4.2 TO BE LIKE GOD

Lucifer's temptation was a variation of the same theme that both Jesus and Adam faced. All shades of the same question. Who will be God? Who will determine the final boundaries of truth? Creature or creator?

Let's unpack this a bit. Lucifer, Adam, and Jesus were each unique creations, all three had a unique "authority" having a "federal headship" over others. Each one of them had to face the test of submission to the will of God. Although we have seen that even though Lucifer was exalted above all other creatures it was not enough for him. He didn't want to remain in his place as merely a created being but to grasp God's power and authority. For Adam, it was to submit to the will of God by denying his wife and refusing to exalt her word over God's. Finally, Jesus was to submit to the will of God, resist taking matters into his own hands, and fulfill God's plans in God's way (see Phil. 2:6ff).

Furthermore, what did it mean to be like God? What did

Lucifer desire? When Lucifer said, "...I will be like the Most High," do we take this to mean that he desired to be like God, loving and benevolent? Let's examine another person who had a close relationship with God, Judas. Judas did not want to become entirely subjected to Jesus, he was not satisfied with being a disciple, a follower, or a learner. Judas was not a spiritual person, nor was he pleased with the message of the Cross. He did not want to serve but became increasingly frustrated by Jesus' refusal to use His powers to inaugurate Israel's national sovereignty, in which he stood to gain much, i.e., political power. As Judas witnessed Jesus foolishly squandering His powers, he came to disdain and scorn Jesus for who He was. Judas was not interested in God or goodness as such, but only in God's power to rule and reign. Judas fell in love with the gifts of God for his purposes, like Simon the sorcerer. So too Lucifer, astoundingly enough, came to despise God for his goodness and loving-kindness. Why? Because the choice that Lucifer made tells us that God's infinite worth and goodness were ultimately deemed worthless and unprofitable by Lucifer who in the final analysis decided to follow his dream, rather than submit to the will of God. Lucifer didn't want the role created for him. He wanted more. A secondary role would never b enough for him. He wanted to exalt his horn over God's horn (God's Son). It is said of him,

> "For you have said in your heart, I will exalt my throne above the stars of God; I will also sit on the mount of the congregation on the farthest sides of the North; I will as-

cend above the heights of the clouds, I will be like the Most High" (Is. 14:13).

So what did he want? Lucifer, like his descendant Judas, wanted two things God possessed (1) autonomy, and (2) power. Leaders need both "might" and "right" to lead. We will look at both aspects before discovering how Lucifer planned to obtain these.

Autonomy (Might) and Authority (Right)

Lucifer wanted to be autonomous from God. He wanted to be independent of God's rule himself. In a strict sense, there is no direct reference in the Bible to the concept of autonomy. Its nearest equivalent comes with the concept of "authority," Greek *exousia*. The Evangelical Dictionary of Biblical Theology states it as follows:

> *"...Authority [automony] is the freedom to decide or a **right** to act without hindrance. All such authority begins with God, for there is no authority except from God (Romans 13:1). God has the right to mold the clay as He wishes (Romans 9:21), and to set times and dates" (Acts 1:17), (Elwell, 45).*

Lucifer wanted to be free from God's authority and live under his authority. He wanted to decide for himself the perimeters of his existence. Once he became vice-regent of the world, that is, the prince of this world, he would move, at will, the ancient boundaries of truth, morality, and ultimately of the very description of reality itself. (We shall consider these matters in a future lesson.) As Lucifer pondered these ideas and was endowed with great gifts, the possibilities were indeed tantalizing. Lucifer, however, had a problem. Authority (or autonomy) without the power to make it effective is worthless. Hence Lucifer needed two things: (1) He needed the ability (power) to make it happen, and (2) He needed the prerogative (the right) to make it happen. For this, he needed subjects and a source of power. The subjects were the men and women of earth and the source of power was the power of death. If he could get the federal head of the human race to sin, then God's justice would have subjected men to his authority. Then he would rule with intimidation, fear, and slavery rather than love, righteousness, and freedom. This understanding makes the freedom of a Christian purchased by Christ a deeper and more profound event. It also helps us to understand why Satan always works to ensnare us in the course of this world with all its personality distortions and destruction. He does not want to see the image of God in man.

Primary and Secondary Gifts

We ask, how could such a plan have been sustained? What made Lucifer think that he could accomplish what he had dreamed? In the light of God's resplendent glory, how could Lucifer have even thought it possible? Here we begin to see the mystery of evil in its true colors. According to our understanding of perfection, it is a state of wholeness in both a religious and ethical sense, and most certainly in a spiritual sense--biblical perfection as we have already stated is an undivided heart. Lucifer trusted in his beauty and thus created within himself a **divided heart**. That is, Lucifer put his faith in his "own beauty," in his "own intellect," and in his "own power" which then resulted in his heart being "lifted." 'Ezekiel 28:17 says this as follows,

"Your heart was lifted up because of your great beauty; You corrupted your wisdom for the sake of your splendor."

Lucifer with full knowledge knew better and yet continued with his plan. The Scriptures reveal Lucifer's tragic demise in Ezekiel 28:17ff, and incredibly we get a glimmer of the nature of evil, which works in the world to this day. It is important to note that Lucifer's position was by appointment. In other words, Lucifer did not work his way to the top of the angelic ladder to become the worship leader or chief "covering cherub, " attributing his authority to his talents and shrewd capabilities. Rather, he was appointed and created expressly for this position. His coverings, his jewels, and his unique position were to reflect the glory of God. Thus Lucifer's chief failure, which led to his heart being lifted (pride), was a failure to recognize his power and beauty were derived and not of his own making and doing. He failed to comprehend his creatureliness and began to believe that he held his powers and anointing by his nature—that he had the gifts inherently. Lucifer established an idol in his heart that separated him from God. In this case, the idol was himself (Ez. 28:1-2). He was the original narcissist, not from any wound but self-deception.

Lucifer's failure to understand that life itself is derived from God, that all life and all reality as created beings is sustained by God. The bestowal of His power and His resources must be seen as a privilege, not as a "right." Lucifer failed to understand that all creatures (men and angels) use God's power (and gifts) in a secondary sense (not in a primary sense) his fall from grace had already begun. Likewise, whenever we appropriate our "spiritual gifts" as our own, trusting in our abilities, we knowingly or unknowingly usurp God's role as the source of all good things and we begin to operate in Satan's realm, thinking and acting just like Lucifer did. Since God says that He will not share His glory with another, we begin to understand the severity of the problem of evil.

Without understanding the essence of Lucifer's crime, the ultimate crime of loving the creature more than the Creator, we will fail to understand the orchestrated efforts of evil to bring sin into the world, foster disobedience to God, and ultimately bring about the man of lawlessness, the antichrist.

Though the spirit of the antichrist has been with mankind, (since Lucifer's fall), he has deceived the nations for one purpose, and for one purpose alone, to rule as a god over all the nations of the earth. He seduces men and women to become lovers of themselves. The number 666 essentially means that when global man deifies himself, fully, portraying the image of his father, the devil, (marked on the forehead (the mind) and the hand (the will), the antichrist will then have come in full measure. the globalization of humanism, or in the deification of man—as being the measure of all things—man will be the chief arbiter of truth and the captain of his destiny, saying in his heart, "I am God!" He will have fleshed out the irrational rantings of a profane and darkened creature saying, "I will ascend to heaven, above the stars of God I will set my throne." In reality, that privilege is predestined for those who love and serve God unconditionally. It is their inheritance, to be transformed into the image and stature of Christ (Ephesians 4:13ff) or to be like God. Let it not be lost that the throne Lucifer once craved will be given to each man or woman who has willingly laid down their own lives. We get the throne of sons, not of rebellious hearts but children of God.

4.3 CONSEQUENCES OF LUCIFER'S REBELLION

The Lord had other plans for this rebellious anointed cherub angel. In Is. 14:12-15 we hear the prophetic voice of God saying, "Yet you shall be brought down to Sheol, to the lowest depths of the Pit. O, Lucifer, son of the morning, how you are cut down to the ground, you who weakened the nations." In his punishment, his great beauty became an abhorrence. Ezekiel 16:25 shows the outcome of abandoning the Lord. God said to Israel after her fall, "Because you trusted in your beauty you made yourself the harlot of all nations and you caused your beauty to be abhorred." In like manner, by abandoning God, Satan was cast away from the source of His beauty and power. God saying in Ek. 28:1, "And I have turned you into ashes on the earth, in all the eyes of all who see you." This reference to ashes is reminiscent of the curse upon the serpent who will crawl on his belly, face in the dust, until his final demise. Lamentations 2:1 and 1:6 respectively show this principle in action,

> "How the Lord has covered the daughter of Zion with a cloud in his anger! He cast down from heaven to the earth the beauty of Israel, and did not remember His footstool in the day of His anger."(NKJV)And from the daughter of Zion, all her splendor has departed. Her princes have become like deer that find no pasture, That flee without strength before the pursuer. (NKJV)

Likewise, the beauty of Lucifer is transformed by the wickedness of his heart and he is cast out of heaven. Revelation 12:3-4 shows the transformation.

> "Then another sign appeared in heaven: an enormous red dragon, with seven heads and ten horns, and seven crowns on his heads."

Jamieson, Fausset, and Brown say, "The fiery red signifies the 'fiery rage' which speaks of Satan's murderous spirit. The seven heads refer to the 'universal dominion' of darkness he will hold throughout the earth, the seven diadems are the counterfeit powers that will simulate the powers of the Holy Spirit" (Jamieson, Fausset, and Brown, 3:693).

Lucifer's name was changed from the son of the morning to Satan the adversary. His position of closeness and intimacy would be lost—estrangement from God was and is his eternal lot, he has become the enemy of God and the things of God. In his transformation, Lucifer loses all the attributes which made him resemble God, his wisdom becomes a cunning strategy, and his heart becomes hardened to love and is filled with hatred, unable to sympathize or empathize with any living being.

In short, Lucifer is "confirmed in evil." For eternity he will be unable to change or repent. Because Satan's knowledge of God's goodness was perfect, God's administration of justice had to be swift, permanent, and commensurate with the crime committed. Satan and all the angels who aligned themselves against the Almighty (a third of the angelic world) were confirmed in evil and are given over to evil until the day of final judgment. Conversely, those angels who decided to be faithful to God, have been confirmed in goodness and can no longer sin, they are called "holy angels" and cannot die.

4.4 THE EVIL EMPIRE

Demons, though enemies of God, remain servants of God. It will become plain in an upcoming lesson that Lucifer, now called Satan, is successful in his attempt to seduce the primordial couple away from God. By their disobedience, he has foolishly relinquished their God-ordained authority to take dominion and govern the earth to the powers of darkness. The devil is now called the Prince of this world, to him, it was granted to "make war with the saints and to overcome them" through the transfer of authority from its vice-regent Adam. To Satan, it was given to rule over every tribe tongue, and nation (Rev 12:11). Jesus identifies Satan as the "ruler of this world" (Rev. 14:30). Paul states that all men and women who live outside of Christ, live according to "...the prince of the power of the air, according to the spirit that is now working in the sons of disobedience" (Eph... 2:1). 1 John 5:19 emphatically states "the whole world lies in the power [under the control] of the evil one." Throughout Scripture, the devil is always seen as the master over an angelic kingdom of supernatural spiritual beings—over fallen angels—which are confirmed in and given over to evil. Revelation 12:7-9 states,

"War broke out in heaven: Michael and his angels fought with the dragon, and the dragon and his angels fought, but they did not prevail, nor was a place found for them in heaven any longer. So the great dragon was cast out, that serpent of old called the devil and Satan, who deceived the whole world: he was cast to the earth, and his angels cast out with him."

Satan's chief method of doing his work was using deception. Satan uses "thrones, principalities, and powers," the collective economy of his kingdom of darkness, in a grand strategy of seduction (Rev 18:23) to keep men enslaved to the kingdom of this world. Therefore God, through the prophetic voice of Paul speaks to us when he says, "Therefore, put on the full armor of

God so that you can take your stand against the devil's schemes" (Eph. 6:11). Sorrowfully, these systems of evil (and man's collusion with them) have been responsible for the misery and sorrows of the family of mankind through the ages. Any experienced missionary can testify of the untold human trauma and grief that has been done to placate and appease these false gods. It is not without merit that the Lord says, "These gods will only bring you sorrow" (Ps. 115:7-8). It only takes a cursory look through history to uncover human sacrificial shrines as people placate their gods. This sorrow lies at the heart of Christian missions.

4.5 THE MYSTERY OF EVIL

Dr. Elwell's Biblical Theology Dictionary says this of sin and evil.

> *Sin involves the refusal of humankind (and angels) to accept its God-given position between the Creator and the lower creation. It flows from decisions to reject God's way, and to steal, curse, and lie simply because that seems more attractive or reasonable. Here we approach the mystery of sin. Why would any creature presume to know more or better than its Creator? The essence of sin, therefore, is not a substance, but a relationship of opposition. Sin opposes God's law, God Himself, and His created beings (Elwell, 739).*

The nature of evil cannot be overstated. Evil is a relationship of opposition and in the philosophical sense the epitome of "unreasonableness." Christians must accept this assessment of evil if we are to make "sense" of much of the inexplicable behavior that occurs in today's world. Dr. Elwell captures the essence of evil. He says,

> *Sin is elusive. Sin has no substance, no independent existence. It does not even exist in the sense that love or justice do. It exists only as a parasite of good or good things. Sin creates nothing, it abuses, perverts, spoils, and destroys the good things God has made. It has no program, no thesis, it only has an antithesis—an opposition. Sometimes wickedness is as senseless as a child who pulls the hair or punches the stomach of another child and then honestly confesses: "I don't know why I did that"* (Elwell, 739).

The senselessness and unreasonableness of sin is its very mystery. How many of us have been confronted with inexplicable behavior of individuals, wringing our hands, shaking our heads saying, "I just don't understand this!" We ask, why this senseless violence? Well, here is the answer. Evil is irrational and senseless—it lacks all judgment. In essence, we cannot find a reason because sin and evil are like an absence rather than a presence. It fails to listen, it walks past the needy, and subsists in alienation rather than making a relationship. In the truest sense, it is the turning away from all good, from the Author of Life, from the source of all that is valid and whole, from the fountainhead of all reality and life—choosing the total abdication of all well-being.

This would not be a great mystery to us if we understood darkness, vice, and death in terms of their opposite—light, goodness, and life. Evil in its fullest dimension is the negation of and separation from the Source of our life. If we see God as Reason, evil then is irrational. If we see God as being Light, evil would be to walk into darkness and blindness. If we see God as being Virtue, evil is vice and we become vicious people, lacking all virtue. However, on the grandest level, if God is the author of reality, of our very life and being, then to turn from Him is to walk directly into unreality, or to walk into non-being or non-life. Sin is in effect, a non-being that leads to death, and his death.

The dynamics of evil consist of opposing tensions that derive from the Evil One's attempt to be ultimately free from the Creator, i.e., the Devil has the will to create (therefore, pride) but not the ability to create (therefore, envy). The degenerating progression is as follows: Envy, then hatred, and then murder. We can see this progression in the fall of the human race, in the relationship between Cain and Abel which ultimately led to Abel's murder. We can see it in biblical history and especially in the Pharisees whose hatred and envy ultimately lead to the murder of Jesus. We can incorporate Judas Iscariot's anger at Mary for wasting Jesus' feet with costly precious, (a form of worship). Inevitably, therefore, envy leads to pride which then leads to murder.

The nature of evil as being antithetical to all that is rational, reasonable, good, and virtuous and having no stated purpose in and of itself is best characterized by the following example. Bernard de Clairvaux is convinced that Lucifer indeed had access to the foreknowledge of God and in doing so, saw his lordship. But Bernard penetratingly asks the question,"...did he not also see his fall?" Bernard of Clairvaux answers cryptically,

> *"For if you foresaw it, what madness was it that made you desire to rule in such misery that you would prefer to be a wretched lord rather than a happy subject? Would it not have been better to be a companion of those who dwell in light than the ruler of those in darkness. Perhaps the vision of your royal rule stuck in your eye like a beam and got in your way so that you could not see your fall?"*

Elwell makes this critically important statement,

> *The question of authority is a fundamental issue facing every person, especially the believer. Furthermore, God has created human beings to live under His authority. When they choose to live under a different rule, that of self or an idol, they sin. This is, in simple summary, the teachings of Genesis 1-3. That portion of the Scriptures illustrates the human tendency, moved by pride, to seek independence from external authority and to establish self as the final authority in life. (Elwell, 45)*

Discussion Questions

1. What are the two things a king must have to rule?

2. Why did Lucifer plan on achieving these two things?

3. What was it that ultimately corrupted Lucifer?

4. What was the thing that finally did him in? And what is the personality disorder that he is the father of?

5. How does Lucifer plan to fill the catacombs of hell in this vein?

Bibliography

Douglas, Robert. Ed. *New Bible Dictionary*. Grand Rapids, MI: Eerdmans, 1962.

Elwell, Walter A. *An Evangelical Dictionary of Biblical Theology.* Grand Rapids, MI: Baker, 1996

Evans, G. R. Ed. *Bernard of Clairvaux, Selected Works.* Western Spiritual Classics. New York: Paulist Press, 1987.

Hodge, Charles. *Systematic Theology*. New York: Charles Scribner and Sons, 1891.

Jamieson, Robert, A.R. Fausset and David Brown.
  A Commentary Critical, Experimental, and Practical on the Old and New Testaments. Grand Rapids: Eerdmans, 1995.

Kittel, Gerhard, *Theological Dictionary of the New Testament.* Grand Rapids, MI: Eerdmans Publishing House, 1967.

CHAPTER FIVE

THE MYSTERY OF NATURAL LAW

As the ultimate artist, the Glory Presence began His outreach with a well-thought-out plan. His objective was to create a world that would reflect His character, His wisdom, His grandeur, and His purposes. He also wanted to make a creature He could lift to Himself with an unspeakable gift of likeness. He wanted to share His love so He would create the world they could live in so they would come to know and love Him. He would create them as free moral agents just as He was. They would be responsible for the earth and their morality under His guidance. He would crown them with dignity and royalty, making them the chief stewards of this new world. Understanding the inherent dangers of creating persons like Himself, but yet not gods, He designed a place that would serve as an object lesson pointing the natural man to spiritual realities, both good and evil. Nature does not only point toward heaven but also points toward death and destruction. These lessons are meant to intrigue man and to provoke him to ask the questions, "What happened?" "What does this mean?"

This story begins as all beautiful stories do with an introductory statement, an explanation of the facts, and then a summary statement. The simplicity of the story underscores its heavenly origin. All other interpretations of this beginning make it far too complicated and in some cases non-biblical. So we begin our study of creation with some simple lessons in composition. This is how we believe you are to read the text.

VS. 1:1 TO BE READ AS AN INTRODUCTION AS A THESIS STATEMENT: "In the beginning, the Glory Presence created the heavens and the earth."

Yes, this is an introductory statement. It is not intended to be read as a creative activity itself but rather as an opening statement. This view is supported by the common sense use of linguistics and the literary style of the Hebrew people.

VS. 1:2 THIS IS TO BE READ AS A PARENTHETICAL CLAUSE: "The earth was without form and an empty waste, darkness was on the face of a very great deep, and the Spirit of God was moving (hovering, brooding) over the face of the waters...." (AMP)

This is the parenthetical clause that describes the setting " ... the earth was without form, an empty waste, and darkness was on the face of a very great deep. The spirit of God was moving (hovering, brooding) over the face of the waters," end of parenthesis.

VS. 1:3 THIS IS TO BE READ AS THE FIRST ACTION: "Then God said, 'Let there be (*hayah*) light.'" (NLT)

This sentence introduces the first creative act. The subsequent events are described linearly: day two, three, and so on. It reads like the good story (history) that it is! Furthermore, like all good masterpieces of literature, it concludes with a summary statement reflecting on the story just told, in Genesis 2:1 (NKJV):

Vs.2:1 THIS IS THE CONCLUSION: "Thus the creation of the heavens and the earth, and all the host of them, were finished." (NKJV)

Hence, there is a beautiful, reasonable development in Genesis 1--an introduction, a setting, a story, and an ending. One can see progressive revelation, action, and then a simple conclusion.

This view is strongly held by Rabbi Rashi, a prominent Hebrew scholar c 1105, (The Parallel Bible Commentary, 7). He considered the *protasis* or the dependent clause to be verse one and saw verse two as the parenthetical clause. He then saw verse three as starting the independent clause, the *apodosis*. This latter view fits with the account of creation being accomplished in six days and does not render the text illogical or confusing. Putting in the punctuation now, it reads:

At the beginning [of his works], God created the heavens and the earth (the earth being without form and void, and darkness was on the face of the deep, and the Spirit of God moved upon the waters) God said, "Let there be light."

This is a story you can tell your children in a profound yet simple childlike way. It is a picturesque language filled with awe and wonder. What will happen next? When will our great-great-great-grandparents appear? What were they like? How did they live? What happened to them? It is a story that needs to resonate deep within our hearts.

5.1 IN THE BEGINNING (Bereshit-7225)

1.1 In the **beginning** God created heaven and earth
1.1 Bereshit bara Elohim et hashamayim ye'et ha'arets.

1.1 At the beginning of his works, God created the heavens and the earth. At a time in which the earth was without form and void, and darkness was on the face of the deep.

The word beginning *(Reshiyth S 7225)* means "the beginning of a period" or the origin of a series of historic acts, hence the following the seven days of creation. A certain period may also indicate this period for the world as we know it, will come to completion, or its end, and then a new period will begin.

5. 2 **Created** (Bara 1254)
1.1 **created** God heaven and earth
1.1 bara Elohim et ha-shamayim ye'et ha'arets.

The introduction follows: the "God(s)" created *(bara S 1254)* the heavens and the earth. *Bara (S 1254)* has the meaning "to split, divide or cut, and or to fashion, bring forth or to create." Many commentators incorrectly say that this means creation out of nothing, but by itself, it does not imply that something was brought into existence out of nothing. Its true value is its use as a "divine work" or a sovereign work of God, which can only be done by God Himself. It is never used about human activity. In other words, men cannot create in the sense of *bara*; only God can create in this larger sense. The Hebrew lexicon defines *bara* as "to shape, fashion, create (always with God as the subject) of heaven and earth, man, of new conditions and circumstances and transformations, of something new, of birth, and miracles." It is thrilling to read these passages with this new understanding: "And he said, Behold, I make *(bara S 1254)* a covenant: before all thy people I will do marvels, such as have not been done in all the earth, nor in any nation: and all the people among which thou art shall see the work of the LORD: for it is a terrible thing that I will do with thee" (Exodus 34:10; see also Isa. 43:1,7,15; 45:7,8,12, 18;48:7; 54:16). How wonderful to know that creation, which has often been explained as a "big bang" was not something natural which somehow randomly or accidentally happened; rather, it was an intentional work of God in a seminal explosion.

5.3 "And God created the heavens and the earth"
1.1 In the beginning God created **heaven and earth**
1.1 Bereshit bara Elohim et **hashamayim** ye'et ha'arets.

The phrase "the heavens" is the term *shamayim (S8064)* in Hebrew. The interesting thing about the word *shamayim* is that it is neither singular nor plural, but dual. Think about this. There are not many words in our culture that speak of "dual realities." Commentators Jamieson, Fausset and Brown say,

> "It is supposed by some commentators to imply the existence of a lower and upper heaven, or of physical and

spiritual heaven—the heaven and the heaven of heavens. By far, in the greatest number of passages in the Bible heaven signifies the dwelling place of the Most High and the abode of the angelic hosts" (Jamieson, Fausset, and Brown, 265-267).

This term included not only the sky in which the birds fly (the atmosphere of the earth) and the stellar skies, but it also included the celestial realms. Paul in the New Testament referred to something called "the third heaven." Paul's understanding looked like this:

Heaven of Heavens (God dwells)
Heavens (Cosmos)
The atmosphere of Earth (The lower part of the cosmos)

The initial term "the heavens and the earth" is an idiomatic expression to signify the entire cosmos or the entire scope of reality including our earth. "Heaven and earth" is a "merism"; a figure of speech that indicates the beginning and the end, as well as everything in the middle. Jamieson, Fausset, and Brown go on to say,

"[The heavens and the earth] denotes the whole material system in germ... not only the sun and its planets, but the fixed stars ... it must include also the various orders of celestial intelligences; for the Hebrews possessed a knowledge of the existence and agency of angels" (Vol 1:2.)

The phrase, in short, includes all the living inhabitants of heaven and earth. The use of this term is problematic for moderns because we are so used to the word "universe." The ancient world had no such term, and certainly, we have no such term in the West for a dual reality. The holistic Hebrew mind, however, could think in such terms.

Thus the Bible begins with a comprehensive cosmology, uniting the visible with the invisible, as well as the temporal and the eternal. It is, therefore, a holistic view and substantial statement of all reality. Scripture begins then with this introductory statement "God, in the beginning, created all things, visible and invisible, and what you are about to read in verses 2-31 is the account of how it happened."

5.4 "And the Earth was without form and void"
Vs. 1:2 and the **earth** was without form and empty
Vs. 1:2 Veha'**arets** hayetah tohu vavohu

"And the earth was without form and void ...." The term "*arets*" (*S776*) means "earth, land, or region." The primary meaning of "*arets*" is earth, whole, and entire. Its use in the initial creation story places it among those items that are universal. Some Jewish scholars say, "*Arets (S776)*" is the creation of the land of Israel only and not the whole planet. If this Jewish idea is true, then the Old Testament is significantly changed; it becomes merely a tribal book for a specific group of people and not for the whole known world. It loses its universal authority. So we reject the Jewish notion and maintain that the "earth" refers to the whole planet.

5.5 "...WITHOUT FORM AND VOID" (TOHU VA BOHU)

The term "without form and void" (Tohu S 8414; Bohu S 922). Tohu alone occurs some 20 times in the Old Testament. It signifies "empty or barren." The OT Hebrew Lexicon describes it as "formlessness, confusion, unreality, emptiness, the formlessness of the primeval earth, as nothingness, or space." Bohu also means "emptiness or nothing, or the void."

The earth was in a state of non-existence (see Isa. 40: 17, 23; 49:4); (Kiel, Vol 1:48). Herman Bavinck, a Dutch Hebrew scholar, says it is tantamount to "space," a state he calls "cosmic formlessness" (100,110). Commentators Jamieson, Fausset, and Brown describe it this way, "The Spirit of God moved or brooded over the vast deep, an abyss of the universal night" (JFB, Vol 1,11). This is in perfect agreement and harmony with what follows in the Genesis creation account where progressive creative acts of God begin with Genesis 1:3 and continue throughout the chapter.

5.6 THE FACE OF THE DEEP (TEHOM S 8415)

Vs. 1.2 and the earth was without form and empty and darkness on the **face of the deep** and the Spirit of God moving gently on the **face of the waters**

Vs. 1.2 Veha'arets hayetah tohu vavohu vechoshech **al-peney tehom** veruach Elohim merachefet **al-peney hamayim.**

Darkness was on the "face of the deep" and "face of the waters" is the Hebrew form of parallelism. The Scriptures are full of this literary technique. Its use is to give further amplification of what the author wishes to convey. The term "face" refers to the idea of surface. The two terms "waters (*hamayim* S 4325) and "the deep" (*tehom* S 8415) are synonymous terms. The "waters" are succinctly tied to what the Bible calls "the deep," or the *tehom* (S 8415) Remembering that the "waters" (*hamayim*) refers to the cosmic oceans or oceans of night, or what the Bible also calls the "*tehom*" (S 8415) or the "deep" the endless oceans of eternal night.

The reading is thus rendered "Nothingness covered the face of the deep, and the Spirit of God hovered gently over this abyss of night." Various definitions are given in the lexicon such as "the deep of subterranean waters," "the primeval ocean," and the "abyss or the grave". "*Tehom*" (S 8415) in the New Testament is translated into "*abussos*" (S 12) wherein the demons begged Jesus to "not command them to go out into the deep," Luke 8:31 (KJV) and Romans 10:7 (KJV), "Who shall descend into the deep?"

The "deep," as in the deep things of God, is the word bathos not *tehom*. The word "*tehom*" (and also "*abussos*") though not physical is nonetheless a geographic place having a deeply spiritual reality. However, we must not see the word *tehom* as space, not even empty space; neither is it a vacuum, but a plane of which may be referred in some sense to the waters of eternity. Ps.18:11 lends further weight to this position, saying, "He made darkness (chosek S 2822) His secret hiding place; as His pavilion (His canopy sukkah S 5521) round about Him were dark waters (*tehom* S 8415) and thick clouds of the skies." Verse 9 says, "He bowed the heavens also and came down, and thick darkness (chosek S 2822) was under His feet" (see also 2 Samuel 22:12; Dt 4:11; and 5:23).

The poetic or symbolic use of the terms darkness, waters, and the deep (including *tohu va bohu*) are designed to convey the state of reality as being absolutely empty, the deafening silence of an immense reality and the same "place" that God dwells. Thus, when God makes the earth, or anything for that matter, from out of the "waters," it is to say that He makes all things out of nothing, indicating *creatio ex nihilo*.

Here is one final note. "Waters" also has a symbolic or spiritual component that must not be overlooked. God has a pattern that is quite discernible—things that are birthed redemptively are always birthed through the water. It is the sign of generation or regeneration that only God can do "bara." Beginning with creation, the waters of a cosmic dimension birth forth the entire cosmos, including man and nature; the waters of the Red Sea birth forth the people of God known as Israel; the water and blood of the side of Christ birthed the new people of God, the church; and finally the waters of baptism are the waters of our spiritual birth. This is a motif in the Scriptures that is everywhere evidenced and consistent with the way God works. Could these be real waters, then? The use of "waters" in the above list shows that they are used figuratively, metaphorically, and also literally in the case of Israel.

5.6 THE SPIRIT OF GOD HOVERED (The Breath of the Gods Ruach Elohim—Strongs #H07307)

1.2 and the earth was without form and empty and darkness on the face of the deep and the Spirit of God moving gently on the face of the waters

1.2 (*Veha'arets hayetah tohu vavohu vechoshech al-peney tehom veruach Elohim merachefet al-peney hamayim.*)

"And the Spirit (breath) of God(s) (Ruach Elohim) hovered (brooded) over the face of the deep."

When the Bible refers to the Spirit of God, the Lexicon defines it as "The third person of the Trinity, coequal, coeternal with the Father and the Son." The Lexicon states that the Spirit imparts warlike energy and gives executive and administrative power. The Spirit endows men with various gifts and the energy of life that is manifested in the *Shekinah* Glory. It is never a depersonalized force. This dynamic Spirit of warlike features hovered or brooded over creation until it brought forth life. This is very similar to the imagery used in the incarnation when the Holy Spirit came upon Mary, also in the inexhaustible burning bush of Moses. At this point, we could say, "The Glory Cloud or wind hovered over the face of the deep."

Adding to our understanding of the word "create" (*bara*: to split and quicken) to the presence of the *Ruach Elohim*, we understand that the primordial role of the *Ruach Elohim* was to bring forth life by separation and division (as in mitosis) and the infusion of life into what it had made. This is what we see happening in the story of Genesis 1. Every time a creative word goes forth from the Word of God (Jesus), the Spirit or Breath of God acts. Thus the process of creation (splitting and quickening) takes place—through the will of the Father, the word of the Son, and the act of the Spirit (Pr. 8:27; John 1:3,10; Eph.... 3:9; Heb.... 1:2; Job 26:13).

The Spirit in His three-fold glory gently hovers like an eagle ... that hovers [*rachaph*] over its young ..." hovers over the formless, empty darkness in which He begins His work as Creator (Dt. 32: 11, NKJV). Here we see a strong, silent, yet deliberate, and gentle movement of the Spirit of Life who is getting ready to give birth to our reality. Psalm 33:7 (NKJV) describes His beginning work as follows, "He gathers the waters of the sea together as a heap; He lays up the deep in storehouses." Our understanding of bara as God splits and cuts and creates comes into play.

Therefore, as we see the Spirit of God hovering over this vastness of nothingness, this *tohu Va bohu*, we know that division (or separation) and quickening is about to begin. The first division (first creative act) begins with "light"; that is, God separates or divides light from the darkness. The Bible calls this first division "day one." What is this light? What is this first creation of God, made by His all-powerful Word, by the hovering and quickening action of the *Ruach Elohim?*

5.8 THE FIRST DIVISION: LIGHT (OHR-S216)

Vs. 1:3 And (Then) said God Let be light and **there was light**,
Vs. 1:3 Vayomer Elohim y**ehi-or-vayehi**
Vs. 1:4 the light that good and separated God between the **light and the darkness,**
Vs. 1:4 Vayar Elohim et ha'or ki-tov vayavdel Elohim beyn **ha'or uveyn ha choshech.**

"Then God said, 'Let there be light; and there was light.' And God saw the light, that it was good; and God divided the light [*ohr* 216] from the darkness [*chosek*]. God called the light Day [*yom*] and the darkness [*chosek 2822*] He called Night" (Gen. 1:3-5, NKJV).

The Holy Spirit's first creation was to divide the dark (*tehom*-the deep) by creating and placing light within it. Second, He divided more of the "waters" (*tehom/the deep*) from the "waters" (*tehom/the deep*) by securing an expanse, or the firmament; He then continues His separating, cutting, and creative work by dividing the seas from the dry land.

But what order of light was this? To understand what this means, we must explore what others have said. Some Biblical scholars say the light refers to Jesus (John 1:1) because Jesus is called the "light of the world." We know that Jesus has eternally been, so this is not talking about His origin. Others say that this refers to moral light. Since we know that moral light is an attribute of God, we know this could not be a "created" substance. Nor does this "light" refer to "elementary principles of light" such as interplanetary cosmic dust and/or radiation because there is no mention of anything of this nature being created; as of yet, there exists no space, no empty space, no time, no universe, no sun, moon or stars. Furthermore, there is some question about whether these particles emit light or are merely reflective of light. What is this light that God made on "day one"? Here is a case where Scripture must explain Scripture. Looking at the Hebrew words used in Genesis chapter 1, we see that there are two words in Hebrew for "light." One is the Hebrew word *ohr* which is used for the creation of the light of the first day; the other is the Hebrew *(Maor S 3974)* used for the light that comes from the sun, moon, and stars of the fourth day. The word *maor* needs to be understood as meaning light-bearer as in light that comes from a candle or lamp as well as light that comes from the sun, moon, and stars. Therefore we see that *ohr* light that is created on day one is different from the light of the sun, moon, and stars. Also, we can say with certainty that this light cannot be God Himself, for this light is a created light and has a tangible reality apart from God. To understand *ohr* type light, we must ask the question, what else does the Bible say about *ohr* light?

> Psalm 104:1-2 (NKJV) "O. LORD my God, You are very great: You are clothed with honor and majesty, Who covers yourself with light [*ohr*] as with a garment."

1 Timothy 6:16 (NKJV) "[God] who alone has immortality, dwelling in unapproachable light [Greek, phos Hebrew *ohr*], whom no man has seen or can see."

Job 38:16-21 (NKJV) "Have you entered the springs of the sea? Or have you walked in search of the depths [*tehom*]? Have the gates of death been revealed to you? Or have you seen the doors of the shadow of death? Have you comprehended the breadth of the earth? Tell Me, if you know all this. Where is the way to the dwelling of light [*ohr*}? And darkness (*chosek*), where is its place, That you may take it to its territory, That you may know the paths to its home?"

Job 26:10 (NKJV) "He drew a circular horizon on the face of the waters, At the boundary of light [*ohr*] and darkness (*chosek*)."

These passages say to us that God wraps himself in this light which is so glorious that mortal man may not even approach it. In the last verse, it is called a "dwelling" which has that mysterious quality of *shekinah* about it. Our true understanding comes from the New Testament "light" *phos* (S 5457), i.e., (Hebrew "*ohr*") which is none other than the light of the angels. In Acts 12:7 we read "Now behold an angel of the Lord stood by him, and a light (*phos*-S5457) shone in the prison and he struck Peter on the side." And in 2 Cor.. 11:14 Satan turns himself into an angel of light (*phos* S 5457). James 1:17 calls God the Father of "lights [S 5457)." The word phos is the root word of our word phosphorous. Phosphorous is the Greek root word for "light-bearer" which is the original, pre-fallen name of Lucifer.

According to these Scriptures, the word *ohr* refers to the celestial light or to the realm in which God dwells, and to the myriad of angels. What He calls "day one" could refer to the making of the celestial light of the heaven of heavens so that when God said, "Let there be light [*ohr*]" He was referring to the commencement of the heaven of heavens—the whole angelic realm—which is sometimes called "the kingdom of heaven." If our understanding of *shamayim* is correct with its dual meaning (both the physical and spiritual reality of heaven) then it is no stretch of the imagination to say that Genesis 1:1 "Let there be light" would reasonably signify the creation and commencement of God's kingdom in and of the heaven of heavens as it extends beyond His three-fold glory.

Job 37:21-23 identifies *ohr*-type light in three ways: light that men cannot look upon, the golden splendor of God Himself, and the garments of God in His awesome majesty. Job 37:22 says that this light comes from God and from the North, so it is the golden splendor of heaven. God speaking in Job 38:19 (NKJV) asks Job, "Where is the way to the dwelling of light *ohr* light?" In other words, "Where do you think light [*ohr*-light] dwells?" This "place of the North" refers to heaven, the throne of God, and it is incidentally the place that Lucifer wanted as his place for his kingdom (Isa. 14: 13-14). Interestingly enough, Rabbinic scholars say that since the fall of man God's glory or light (*ohr*) is only manifested in the Torah. The root word *ohr* can be seen in the word Torah. Menorah (candlestick) is also derived from the word *ohr*.

Augustine says in the City of God,

> *When Scripture speaks of the creation of the world, it does not indicate clearly whether, or in what order, the angels were created. If they are alluded to at all, it is perhaps under the name of the heavens ... or, more likely, under the term light (XI:215). Further support for this perspective is found in the Scriptures. It is generally understood that the throne of God and the abode of angels is "in the heaven of heavens." Heaven is God's dwelling place according to Psalm 11:4 and is also the abode of the angels in which they behold the unveiled glory of the Lord (Matt. 18:10).*

Therefore, returning to Genesis 1:3, we understand that when God spoke for the very first time His light (the light of His glory) was revealed and made manifest resulting in the creation of the first reality out of the darkness of emptiness; it was made out of "the nothing" from the depths of eternity. It was the creation of the heaven of the heavens and all its angelic hosts.

5.9 THE FIRMAMENT

Then God said, "Let **there be a firmament** (rakia 7554) in the midst of the waters and let it divide the waters from the waters. Thus God made the firmament and divided the waters which were under the firmament from the waters which were above the firmament; and it was so. And God called the firmament Heaven" (Gen. 1:6-8, NKJV).

Vs. 1.6 Vayomer Elohim **yehi rakia** *betoch hamayim vyhi mavdil beyn mayim lamayim.*

Leaning on our new understanding of "waters" as referring to the oceans of nothingness, we learn that they are divided by the firmament or by an expanse. What is this expanse? The firmament cannot refer to the *terra firma* because the earth itself is not created until the third day; therefore, "Firmament" must mean something else. We get our understanding by exegeting the Hebrew word rakia which is the root word "firmament" when translated into English. It means that which is fixed and steadfast rather than that which is firm or solid.

Girdlestone states this in the following remarkable comment.

> *The application of this word to the heavenly bodies is simple and beautiful; they are not fickle and uncertain in their movements but are regulated by a law that they cannot pass over ... The firmament, then, is that which is spread or stretched out, hence an expanse ... [or] two ideas to the term, namely, [as rendered in the LXX] extension and fixity, or (to combine them in one) fixed space (Girdlestone, 268-9).*

We understand that *rakia* explains the universe, or the vast expanse of the starry or stellar skies, which we know from science to be 16.2 billion light-years across. Job 26:7 (KJV) reemphasizes two points: First, "He [God] **stretcheth** out the North [northern sky] over the empty place, and second, He [God] hangeth the earth upon nothing." The "empty place" refers to the "abyss" or the "oceans of nothingness" upon which the firmament is hung or fixed.

The Hebrew word *rakia,* derived from the verb *raka*, means to spread out. For instance, this verb is found in Job 37:18 (KJV), "Hast thou with him spread out [*raka*] the sky, which is strong, and as a molten looking glass?" Isaiah 45:12 (KJV) says, " ...I, even my hands, have stretched out [raka] the heavens ..., " "Mine hand also hath laid the foundation of the earth, and my right hand hath spanned [raka] the heavens ..." (Is. 48:13, KJV). Psalm 136:6 (KJV), "To Him that stretched out [*raka*] the earth above [or over] the waters...." Robert Girdlestone states this beautifully as follows:

> *"The interplanetary spaces are measured out by God, and, though the stars are ever moving, they generally preserve fixed relative positions; their movements are not erratic, not in straight lines, but in orbits, and thus, though ever-changing, they are always the same" (Girdlestone, 269).*

Therefore, we see a major separation or division in the heavenlies: the celestial beings live beyond the firmament, beyond what man can explore which is separated by the cosmic oceans called the waters of eternity. Beyond this air is the dwelling of God who is "[God] dwelling in unapproachable light, whom no man has seen or can see ... " (1 Tim. 6:16, NKJV). God's throne, then, is beyond the fixed heavens.

Ezekiel 1:25 (NKJV): "A voice came from above the firmament that was over their heads...."

Ezekiel 1:26 (NKJV): "And above the firmament over their heads was the likeness of a throne, in appearance like a sapphire stone; on the likeness of the throne was a likeness with the appearance of a man high above it."

Robert Girdlestone says in *Synonyms of the Old Testament*,

> *...For where our intellect ceases to operate and fails to find a limit to the extension of space, here faith comes in; and whilst before the eye of the body there is spread out an infinity of space, the possession of a super-material [or supernatural] nature brings us into communion with a Being whose nature and condition cannot adequately be described by terms of locality or extension. The heavens and the heaven of heavens cannot contain Him; the countless stars are not only known and numbered by Him but are called into existence and fixed in their courses by His will and wisdom (Girdlestone, 266).*

5.10 THE WORD OF GOD (dabar-Yahweh)

This principle of separation and division is the operating principle for all subsequent days of creation which indicates successive acts of division by God as He creates. As such, they are not "time categories." The "days of creation" then indicate division or separation in the creative work of God (as opposed to indicating time) which were accomplished at the moment He said, "Let there be ...." These words "Let there be..." speak to the doctrine of God's omnipotence. Dr. Hodge helps us to understand the correct biblical doctrine of power using the following quote.

"We get the idea of power from our own consciousness. That is, we are conscious of the ability to produce effects. Power in man is confined within very narrow limits. We can change the current of our thoughts, or fix our attention on a particular object and we can move the voluntary muscles of our body. Beyond this our direct power does not extend. It is from this small measure of efficiency that all the stores of human knowledge and all the wonders of human art are derived. It is only our thoughts, volitions, and purposes, together with certain acts of the body, that are immediately subject to the will. For all other effects, we must avail ourselves of the use of means. We cannot will a book, a picture, or a house into existence. The production of such effects requires protracted labor and the use of diverse appliances."

It is by removing all limitations of power, as it exists in us, that we rise to the idea of the omnipotence of God. We can do very little. God can do whatever He pleases. We, within very narrow limits, must use means to accomplish our ends. With God means are unnecessary. He wills, and it is done. He said, "Let there be light" and there was light. He, by his volition, created the heavens and the earth. In the New Testament, we see similar phenomena. At the volition of Christ, the winds ceased and there was a great calm. By an act of the will He healed the sick, opened the eyes of the blind, and raised the dead. This simple idea of the omnipotence of God, that He can do without effort and by volition whatever He wills, is the highest conceivable idea of power; and it is that which is presented in the Scriptures (Hodge, 392).

What is in focus is the word of God speaking. Thus, when Scripture says, "...And God saw that it was good" it speaks of a miraculous and yet substantial creation; not a mere illusion or a dream, but real substantive work, with parts, with quality, and with life. It also speaks of an immediate creation being called into being as it is spoken. Psalm 147:15 also demonstrates this principle.

In keeping with the integrity of the universe and domain of the word dabar, the acts of creation—the next divisions of the creation account—would be successive but immediate. At every stage, God's omnipotent Word would be manifested (creating reality) since this is the very nature of dabar. This word carries power within itself. For God to speak is to declare, to cause, the fulfillment of the thing spoken. The etymology of this word is illuminating as to its meaning. Here is an excerpt from the Theological Wordbook of the Old Testament to help us understand further:

> "As a verb, this word generally denotes the producing of whatever the same word means as a noun, hence: to speak, declare, warn, threaten, command, promise, sing..., etc. The noun always denotes a message or at least a verbal unit that came from contemplative thought, or most matters about moral and ideal values."

Jamieson, Fausset, and Brown say this about "let it be":

> *"This phrase, which occurs so repeatedly in the account means: willed, decreed, appointed; and the determining will of God was followed in every instance by an immediate result. Whether the sun was created at the same time with, or long before, the earth, the dense accumulation of fogs and vapors which enveloped the chaos had covered the globe with a settled gloom. But by the command of God, the light was rendered visible; the thick murky clouds were dispersed, broken, or rarefied, and light diffused over the expanse of waters. The effect is described in the name "day," which in Hebrew signifies "warmth," "heat"; while the name "night" signifies a "rolling up," as night wraps all things in a shady mantle" (JFB, Vol 1, 6).*

What we understand here is that when God says, "Let there be!" a corresponding action occurs. An immediate creation with its divisions is a framework that would be in line with the integrity of the universe and with the totality of the Bible: Scripture clearly states that the world and all its ages were formed in six creative days, divisions, or stages (Ex.... 20:11, 31:17). There was no point in which matter, nor anything else, spontaneously generate itself without the created Word of God has spoken it into being. Matter is powerless to produce. It only possesses a capacity for obedience (*potentia obedientialis*) not the capacity to generate life (JFB, Vol 1:7). It takes life to generate life. We shall see this more clearly when we consider the creation of the third day.

5.11 "EVENING AND MORNING....DAY ONE"

"And there was evening (*ereb* 6153) there was morning (*baqar* 1239)—day one."

Of great significance is the phrase "and there was evening and there was morning, day one." Important to note that there is no measure of time (solar time) as of yet. There are no moon, sun, or stars. Many commentators say that this "evening and morning" phrase refers to the Hebrew method of dating. The Hebrew "day" or "*yom*" refers to a day that begins in the evening and goes until the following morning.

"All birth," said Shelling, "...is from darkness into light. All origins are wrapped in obscurity. If no one tells us who our parents and grandparents are or were, we do not know them" (Bavinck, 127).

The story of our creation begins in this darkness, or waters, which is a sort of metaphysical chaos. God is moving "nothing" into something in the creation account. He is the author of a story, and so He begins by moving from darkness into light.

From this perspective, light stands for bringing into existence (to give birth—*dar luz*—to give light) bringing light and especially goodness into being; this is why He follows all days but one with "and God saw that it was good." Darkness stands for uncreated reality because the deep formlessness of nothingness called "night," "morning" or "the day" would refer to something that has been created and can be seen and of which God can say, "It is good." The parallelism would be something like this:

Darkness to Light
Nothing (abyss) to Something (light)
Night to Day
Evening to Morning
Chaos and Formlessness to Order and Existence.

God is merely following a faithful pattern seen everywhere in the Bible where we begin in darkness and move toward the light. Faith likewise begins in darkness. Our journey (born in sin/darkness) moves from dark to light, from disorder to order, from sin to holiness.

The second phrase "one day" must also be broken down into two parts. Let us begin with the word "day" or *"yowm"* in Hebrew. There are various ways it can be used: a working day, a day's journey; days, lifetime (pl.); time, period (general); year; temporal references; today; yesterday; tomorrow. When it is used with a cardinal number it always refers to 24 hours. When it is used with an ordinal number, it refers to the order or sequential activity, not a 24-hour day. A cardinal number tells "how many." Cardinal numbers are also known as "counting numbers" because they show quantities such as 8 puppies or 14 friends. Ordinal numbers tell the order of things in a set—first, second, third, etc. Ordinal numbers do not show quantity. They only show rank or position such as third fastest or sixth in line. The Scriptures (except day one) use ordinal numbers to describe the creation events, which means that these can refer to acts, divisions, or sequential events, not necessarily 24 hours, and in fact, it is most likely not a 24 time. Let us however look at what Jamieson, Fausset, and Brown say about "day one":

"The first day, day one, for the cardinal number is used, not the ordinal number, first." And the clause translated should stand thus: 'And the evening was and the morning was one day.' In the account of all the successive creations, the days are mentioned by the ordinal numbers, as "second, third, etc... But here the language is singular, and it has been shrewdly conjectured that the use of the cardinal for the first day may have been adopted to show that the existence of a day then was not an occurrence out of the course of nature, but only that one

103

was singled out and particularized as a starting point for the rest."

Whether or not Jamieson, Fausset, and Brown agree with the shrewd usage of this construction or not will be known, but surely it is meant to be clearer than this presentation. We are left with a mystery. What do you think of this singular change?

What does Scripture say about this "one day?" "For a thousand years in thy sight are but as yesterday when it is past, and as a watch in the night." It also says, "... that one day is with the Lord as a thousand years and a thousand years as one day." Does the use of this one day imply 24 hours? The time may be less than 24 hours.

5.12 THE THIRD DIVISION..."Creation of the Dry Land"

Vs.1:9 "Then God said, 'Let the waters under the heavens be gathered together into one place and the let the dry land appear and it was so.'"

Vs.1:9 Vayomer Elohim yikavu hamayim mitachat hashamayim el-makom echad vetera'eh hayabashah vayehi chen.

Genesis 1:9 and the following verses begin the creation account dealing with the actual earth and describe it in three phases:

1) With the division of the dry land from out of the waters underneath the heavens, He gathered into one place to form to create the seas.

2) By the calling forth of the dry land, by having it appear from the waters, separating the dry land from the waters

3) By clothing with a garment or covering the dry land with (a) green grasses and plants, (b) seed-yielding herbs and plants, and (c) fruit-bearing trees including all trees and shrubs bearing fruit in which there is a seed according to its kind, that is, a fruit kernel.

Keeping with the motif that the works of God are birthed out of water, we look to 2 Peter 3:5 when it says, "The earth was formed out of water and by means of water." Genesis 1:9 states that God "gathered together into one place" the "waters" previously talked about under the heavens, revealing that the planet originated in a completely fluid state from which the earth would subsequently be formed. What is in mind is a gathering together of the waters of potential creation into a heap which is now material and visible to the human eye. There is in this moment a creation of the waters out of the waters of the abyss or the oceans of the cosmic seas where the divine omnipotent "hand of God" swept or "hewn out" creation of something out of nothing as in Ps. 95:5: "His hands formed the dry land."

From other Scriptures, we are told that there was a time (or a state) in which the mountains had not yet been brought forth

(Prov. 8:24-5) which indicates a state in which there was no topography, i.e., no canyons, streams, rivers, bluffs, plateaus, etc. From 2 Samuel 22:16, we get a further description of what the "foundations of the earth" really are. Foundations generally refer to the depths (floor) of the oceans, crust, and core of the earth. This leads us to believe that the whole globe may at one time have been fluid. But there is also a theological reason that the earth is birthed out of water, and that is that all births which are initiated through God's initial power are birthed in water: the birth of Israel through the Red Sea, birth through the amniotic fluid, the new birth from the waters of baptism and even the new people of God who inherited the Promise Land crossing the Jordan, another type of baptism. Dr. Bavinck says, "All of life's [creation's] processes were aroused by the Divine Word of power and animation of the Spirit" (Bavinck, 104).

God's omnipotent power applied creative pressure (as in the Artist's touch) and caused divine energy to both make and fashion matter simultaneously, dividing the metals (iron, copper magnesium, and nickel) of the earth from the softer silicates. He formed the earth's covering (sand crust) and core at once, though perhaps some time would be needed for cooling. It is important to note that the core of the earth is still liquid or fluid and very hot. Dt. 32:22 says, "For a fire is kindled in My anger, and shall burn to the lowest hell; It shall consume the earth with her increase, and set on fire the foundations of the mountains."

The importance of this process is significant and prophetic (eschatological) for the following reason. In keeping with the typologies and symbolism of the Bible, we understand that the physical world is a picture of the spiritual world or an invisible reality. The formation and creation of the earth were no different. Often, modern scholars deride the primitive understanding of the ancient peoples as ignorance, but the spiritual reality of such things was not lost on them. For them, the underworld (Sheol) is pictured as being in the "center of the earth or under the waters" as in Job 26:5-6 where it says,

> "The dead tremble, Those under the waters and those inhabiting them. Sheol is naked before Him and destruction has no covering."
>
> "As for the earth, from it comes bread, but underneath, it is burned up as by fire" (Job 28:5).

Numbers 16:30 shows the upper and lower realities, i.e., physical reality and its likeness to the spiritual reality:

> But if the Lord creates a new thing, and the earth opens its mouth and swallows them up with all that belongs to them and they go down alive to the pit, then you will understand that these men have rejected the Lord." And it came to pass, as he finished speaking all these words, that the ground split apart under them, and the earth opened its mouth and swallowed them up... So they and all those with them went down alive into the pit; the earth closed over them and they perished from among the assembly.

Proverbs 15:24 says The way of life is above the wise, that he may depart from hell beneath." Isaiah 14:9 says, "Hell from beneath you is excited about you, to meet you at your coming; it stirs up the dead for you...the maggot is spread under and worms cover you.

The spiritual layers are often replicated in temporal terms so that we can easily make the association: physical heaven with the spiritual heaven, physical stars with angelic beings, earth, the abode of man, beneath the earth as the place of demons, deserts with spiritual aridity. We can therefore see that the formation and creation of the earth was not a "cosmic" accident; rather, it was a well-planned object lesson that would serve God's people well to communicate "transcendent" truths, not primitive superstitious folklore. Thus when God begins the separation of the waters from the dry land, He brings forth the earth as we know it today when he says, "Let the dry land appear and it was so...and God called the dry land Earth." In apportioning the waters, he creates the atmosphere of the earth. They are integrally related (atmospheric pressure and depths of the oceans) as seen in Job 28:24-27:

For He looked to the ends of the earth and seeth under the whole heavens; To make the weight of the winds, and he weigheth the waters by measure...Then did he see it, and declare it, he prepared it, yea, and searched it out.

At the establishment of the ocean's perimeters, (spreading out of the ocean floors, i.e., the foundations) the earth gave birth to mountain ranges all along the coastlines of the various continents; thermal contractions occurred in the earth, bringing forth the hills and valleys. The weight and accuracy of this description are embedded in the word "formed" (*chil*) which elsewhere means to bring forth (in pain). In Dt. 32:18, we see an even more profound sense of this word *chil*: "Of the Rock who begot you, you are unmindful, and have forgotten the God who fathered (*chil*) you." This speaks of Jesus as our Rock and the pain that He endured to "bring forth" the redeemed (Gal 4:19). See also when Moses was instructed to "hit" the rock rather than speak to the rock. The implication is that the living water which flows from Jesus to His own was birthed in pain (*chil*).

As the mountains rose, the waters subsided, cooling the earth and establishing an even temperature on the planet itself. Jamieson, Fausset and Brown say, "...The globe must have been of necessity the theatre of various catastrophes, by which the uniform crust of the earth was raised above the waters, and a state of things established analogous to that which geography now presents to us" (Vol 1:11). We see this process clearly in Psalm 104:6-7 that gives an allusion to the creative drama (see the whole Psalm). Since it is set within the context of the creation of the heavens and earth, we have biblical authority to use this Psalm at this point rather than apply it to the flood narrative.

The waters stood above the mountains, At Your rebuke they fled; At the voice of your thunder, they hastened away. They went up over the mountains, They went down into the valleys, to the place which You founded for them. You have set a boundary that they may not pass over, That they may not return to cover the earth [of their own accord] (Ps. 104:6-7).

Astounding as this is, all of this happened on day three. The universe of the sun, moon, and stars had not even been born yet. The light of God's countenance sustained and preserved the non-sentient forms of life at this initial stage. The light of the sun will soon become the way through which His grace (sustaining power) is mediated. Scripture alludes often to the sun as a temporal object signifying God Himself. Psalm 19 shows the typology of the sun, appearing as an object lesson for His light (His face) which will someday swallow up all the firmament and earth into His glory. Light and darkness at this stage still reveal the uncompleted work of salvation. Let us read it:

THE HEAVENS declare the glory of God, and the firmament shows and proclaims His handiwork. 2 Day after day pours forth speech, and night after night shows forth knowledge. 3 There is no speech nor spoken word [from the stars]; their voice is not heard. 4 Yet their voice [in evidence] goes out through all the earth, their sayings to the end of the world. Of the heavens God has made a tent for the sun, 5 which is as a bridegroom coming out of his chamber; and it rejoices as a strong man to run his course. 6 It's going forth is from the end of the heavens, and its circuit to the ends of it; and nothing [yes, no one] is hidden from the heat of it.

THE GENESIS TOUCH

The nugget of truth given in this passage is that the heavens declare and point to supra-reality which is unseen by fallen man. Once again we see a world in which everything in it has been designed to provide man with a "cubby hole" to see the spiritual reality of sin, evil, darkness, and light. All things belonging to life, light, and goodness proclaim His economy, the kingdom of God, while those things belonging to the world of darkness, death, fragmentation, and decay point to the spiritual problem of mankind. The entire cosmos is one big object lesson for fallen man who is blind to the spiritual life and truly "gropes" his way in the darkness. Day after day, night after night, though there is no speech nor voice heard, they have given evidence that light exists, angels dream, and paradise awaits mankind. Take a moment to think about this: our planet is the only thing of color in the universe (Borman. The American Experience—The Saturn Trip).

The final touch is in the creation of the sun, which God has made as a "bridegroom coming out of his chamber." This points to the consummation of a marriage. Upon the union completion, the bridegroom exits with arms upraised and a smile that explodes—indicating that the festal victory has occurred within the bridal chamber. The bride has been "taken." The seminal explosion which has just occurred is a mini-portrait of the seminal explosion of creation in a singular event of creation. The seminal fluid explodes into all parts of the cosmos, and the bridegroom comes out of the chamber celebrating victory. The temporal-created sun "bursts" into the morning and brings with it light into the dark again. Each time a bridegroom experiences this explosion he reenacts the original sign of creation, like a little "god" enacting the image of God in man. There will come a day in which the shadows upon this earth will disappear, and the festal celebration will begin in perpetual light, goodness, and glory.

The chronology of the Mosaic record has long been a subject of debate and considerable scorn by modern scholars due to the record listing the creation of plant life before the creation and placement of the sun. Jamieson, Fausset and Brown say,

"Now we know that the prime mission of vegetation is physical, the removal from the atmosphere of a deadly gas (carbonic acid), and the supply to it of one eminently support of life (oxygen). It is conceivable that the earth was still in formation as the trees and vegetation were being placed upon its surface, taking underground its various forms of plant life, as the earth's surface was being further molded and defined. This vegetation sub-served another important purpose in developing coal deposits beneath the earth. It is important to note that again the miracle process of creation extends not only to the inanimate features of the earth but also to the tender shoots of vegetation" (1:8).

Professors Keil and Delitzsch make the following startling observation:

"...we must not picture the work of creation as consisting of the production of the first tender germs which were gradually developed into herbs, shrubs, and trees; on the contrary, we must regard it as one element in the miracle of

creation itself, that at the word of God not only tender grasses, but herbs, shrubs, and trees, sprang out of the earth, each ripe for the formation of blossom and the bearing of seed and fruit, without the necessity of waiting for years before the vegetation created was ready to blossom and bear fruit. Even if the earth was employed as a medium in the creation of the plants since it was God who caused it to bring them forth, they were not the product of the powers of nature, generatio aequivoca *in the ordinary sense of the word, but a work of divine omnipotence, by which the trees came into existence before their seed, and their fruit was produced in full development, without expanding gradually under the influence of sunshine and rain" (Vol 1:11).*

All of this happened on day three of creation. The formation of the earth, rocks, craters, and other physical features, as well as the oceans and seas, are all pieces of evidence of real creation. We must not picture this creation as instantly appearing as in some "magical poof," as a figment of emanation from the mind of God, but that creation was truly real and truly made. It began as soon as God spoke and continued until it was completed, or until it became "morning," all of it occurring within the timelessness of eternity. This does not mean that the world is eternal, as God is eternal, but simply that its "beginning" was outside of 24 hours.

Nonetheless, because parts of creation take place outside of "normal time" they are still considered "instantaneous," which is a misnomer, for they precede the moment, as in the instantaneous curing of organic diseases by Jesus. Since God is the ever-present I am, we deduce that action for God consists in the ever-present "Eternal Now." What would that look like? For man, and everything under the heavens, there is a purpose and a time. "To every purpose, there is a time and a judgment" (Eccl.8:6). God says of Himself, "I a*m the First, I am also the Last." He is both at once the First and the Last.*

Continuing, God says, "I have not spoken in secret from the beginning; From the time that it was, I was there." In this divine dimension, we cannot talk about time, but we can talk about a state of being—the Ever-Present Now, and the Ever-Present is. As Creator, whenever He imposes His Word and His will upon the created sphere, He creates. God is not limited by time or space. Dr. Bavinck says,

> "The calling forth of the mountains does not require any extension or diffusion through space but is an immediate 'obedience' by matter. All that occurred in verse 9 occurs in temporal and spatial freedom" (Bavinck, 77).

In other words, creation doesn't have to crawl through time. It is supra-temporal. This would be and is the definition as well as the background (basis) of the miraculous.

5.13 The Fourth Division: The Sun, Moon, and Stars

Genesis 1: 14 Then God said, "Let there be lights in the expanse of the heavens to separate the day from the night, and let them be for signs and seasons and days and years. And let them be for lights in the expanse of the heavens to give light on the earth, and it was so. And God made the two great lights, the greater light to govern the days and the lesser light to govern the night. He made the stars also.

Vs. 1:14 Vayomer Elohim yehi meorot birekia hashamayim lehavdil beyn hayom uveyn halaylah vehayu leotot ulemoadim uleyamim veshanim.

God's purpose for the light bodies we see in the sky was so that life might thrive in the waters, in the air, and on the dry land. In the fourth division, light (*maor*) bodies received a threefold purpose: (1) "to divide between the day and the night" or to govern the day and night" and (2) "to serve as signs to mark seasons and days and years" and (3) to "serve for lamps" or "lights in the expanse of the sky to give light (*maor* light) on the earth" (Kiel and Delitzsch, Vol 1, 56).

The record of Genesis clearly says that God also made the stars. This must mean all the stars and all the galaxies in our expanding but fixed universe, not only the planets in our solar system or the stars in our galaxy; but all stars everywhere. We are looking at the creation of all the galaxies that exist and have existed as well as all of the innumerable stars created at immeasurably great distances from each other. God made them all!

But we ask, how did He do this? What was the relationship of the already existing earth to the universe in all its splendor being created on the fourth day? John Gribbin in Cosmic Coincidences, Dark Matter, Mankind, and Anthropoid Cosmology describes the relationship of all things such as the size of the stars, the rate of expansion, and the material in the universe that occupies space between the stellar clusters known as galaxies. He has discovered that the most distant stars which are now old and dying out have a bearing on the continued existence of life on earth. Each part of the universe affects and preserves the rest. But is there a specific and theological reason for the creation of the stars?

5.14 THE FIFTH DIVISION, BIRDS AND SEA CREATURES

Genesis 1:20 "Then God said, 'Let the waters **teem** with swarms of living creatures, and let birds fly above the earth in the open expanse of the heavens.' And God created the great sea monsters, and every living creature that moves, with which the waters **swarmed** after their kind; and every winged bird after its kind; and God saw that it was good."

1:20 Vayomer Elohim yishretsu hamayim sherets **nefesh chayah** *ve'of yeofef al-ha'arets al-peney rekia hashamayim.*

Notice the emphasis on the words "teem" and "swarms." It does not state that only a single pair were created of each kind and they by natural means propagated to an abundant level. On the contrary, the words, "Let the waters teem with swarms of living creatures..." (Gen. 1:20, NAS) boldly state that large numbers of individual kinds and species were made. Although rich in variety at its original creation, differentiation has continued to occur in all mammalian and plant life. For instance, the bear family genus may have only been a few kinds of "bears" while today we have a variety (of species) within the bear genus known as the "polar, black, brown, koala, grizzly, etc." The same would be true of the dog family. Today's dog family includes cocker, boxer, shepherd, collies, poodles, hounds, etc. Yet at the original creation, the sub-species or lower divisions of a class had not yet been differentiated. But the effect of the blessing would ensure that the earth would continue to "be fruitful and multiply" as further described in this quote: Human beings were the only ones created singly; for the unity of the human race has a very different signification from that of the so-called animal species (Kiel and Delitzsch, 61).

5.15 THE SIXTH DIVISION; ANIMALS AND MAN

Genesis 1:21 "Then God said, Let the earth bring forth living creatures after their kind: cattle and creeping things and beasts, out of the earth after their kind; and it was so. 1:22 God [thus] created the great sea monsters, along with every particular species of living thing that crawls, with which the waters teem, and every particular species of winged flying creature. God saw that it was good."

Vs. 1:21 Vayivra Elohim et-hataninim hagedolim ve'et kol nefesh hachayah haromeset asher shartsu hamayim leminehem ve'et kol-of kanaf leminehu vayar Elohim ki-tov.

After the sea, waters and air are filled with living creatures, Genesis 1:24-25 tells us how the Word of God now goes to the earth to produce the land animals after their kind. There are three classes that God created, each "after its kind": (1) the cattle, which also denote larger land animals; (2) the creeping animals, including insects, reptiles, and worms; and (3) the beasts of the earth, which denote the freely roving animals. The fact that each is created "after its kind" is repeated for emphasis in verse 25: "And God made the beast of the earth according to its kind, cattle according to its kind, and everything that creeps on the earth according to its kind. And God saw that it was good."

5.16 THE CREATION OF MANKIND

1:26 "God said, 'Let us make man with our image and likeness. Let him dominate the fish of the sea, the birds of the sky, the livestock animals, and all the earth — and every land animal that walks the earth.'"

Vs. 1:26 Vayomer Elohim na'aseh adam betsalmenu kidemutenu veyirdu bidegat hayam uve'of hashamayim uvabehemah uvechol-ha'arets uvechol-haremes haromes al-ha'arets.

1:27 "God [thus] created man with His image. In the image of God, He created him, male and female He created them."

1:27 Vayivra Elohim et-ha'adam betsalmo betselem Elohim bara oto zachar unekevah bara otam.

The creation account now leads us to the culmination of God's creative acts. All of it leads to and is made for what follows in Genesis 1:26-27, the creation of mankind in God's image and likeness, making man male and female. When God begins to create people in His image, the author of Genesis shifts from the "let there be" mode of speaking (used in verses 3-25) to what Hebrew grammarians call the "plural of majesty." This plural form of expression is best explained as a plural of self-deliberation. Rightly understood, this way of speaking expresses not so much the "plural of majesty" as the "majesty of God's plurality." Through this phrase, God is expressing that He is entering into an act with the fullness of the three beings of the God-head. He is also entering in with the fullness of His plurality and personality which would suit the creation of people who will be made in His image and likeness.

There remain three puzzling phrases in these texts that beg for definition. The phrases "It is good," "God blessed it," and "God rested from his works."

5.17 IT IS GOOD

Vs. 1:31 "God saw all that he had made, and behold, it was very good. It was evening and it was morning, the sixth day."

Vs. 1:31 Vayar Elohim et-kol-asher asah vehineh-tov me'od vayehi-erev vayehi-voker yom hashishi.

On all days, except the second day, God looks at what He has made and pronounces it "good." The word *towb* (S 2896) can have three meanings, (1) a good, agreeable, pleasant thing, (2) a thing which is of moral goodness and ought to bring forth and promote welfare, and (3) a sign of His bounty. By far, the use of this word is in the domain of "beauty." The things that God has made are beautiful (Brown, Driver, Briggs and Gesenius, *towb*). These created things are made for His pleasure, and He finds them beautiful. He declares the creation of everything He had made as "very good," or very beautiful. There is a correlation between this statement and the statement "the beauty of holiness" that would not be too far from its original meaning. The wholeness and extraordinariness of what has been done can be called so perfect and so good as to be beautiful and holy. The reason that this is important is that the major attack of the devil is to mar, smirch, destroy, distort and dismiss the beauty of creation, not only in nature but especially in man himself.

THE GENESIS TOUCH

The story now takes a closer more detailed look at the creation of mankind. The earth is still an undressed ball (day 4) when God begins to think forward to the creation of His special creature, man and woman, two people who would best represent His character on earth. Man was to represent Him by being the overseer, protector, and provider—God endowed Adam with those kingly attributes. Woman was to represent His tender, reproductive, caregiver, companion, and submissive attributes—the queenly attributes which were fulfilled fully in the character of the Son and the Spirit. God's fullness required two people to display His glory. From their love would arise, children, which represent the glorious emergence of the Holy Spirit as a result of their deep and intimate fellowship. The three aspects of man would best reflect the fullness of God's being materially. In this, we see complexity but unity.

The Genesis creation account is a beautiful document of utter simplicity and wholeness. It is first historical (it does not give us a legend), and it is miraculous; miracles cannot be grounded or explained in the reality in which we live. Miracles exist above our time-space reality; they have their source in eternity, and they are possible and do happen on earth, in space, and in time because such reality exists. Miracles are not subject to natural laws, and that is why they are called "miracles" as compared to the other works of God, which are done in time, process, and development we frequently call natural law. Even "natural law" is not self-operating, self-sustaining, but is upheld, maintained, and preserved in perfect order and harmony by God Himself.

Discussion Questions

1. Discuss the simple construction of any good story which starts with an introduction (thesis), the story, and then the conclusion. Can you see or identify these principles in the first and second chapters of Genesis?

2. Why do conservative scholars have to insist upon creation taking place in verse one? How does this view of Rabbi Rashi put that to rest? Please define and illustrate the "construct" theory (in the making) vs. the "absolute" theory (already done)?

3. "In the Beginning" has both a quantitive and qualitative dimension to it. What are those dimensions? Why is this important theologically and in terms of creation itself?

4. What mystery did you discover about the term *"shamayim"*? How does that affect you theologically, and is it believable? What mystery about "let there be light" reflects the possibility of the creation of God's throne and angels?

5. If our rendering of a simple story is true then can you see the three heavens of St. Paul (the heaven of heavens, the cosmos, and the atmosphere) described in the initial creation story?

Bibliography

Arnold, Bill. T. *Encountering Genesis*. Grand Rapids, MI: Baker Book House, 1998.

Bavinck, Herman. *In the Beginning*. Grand Rapids, MI: Baker Book House, 1999.

Brown, Driver, Briggs, and Gesenius. *The Brown-Driver-Briggs Hebrew and English Lexicon*. Peabody Mass: Hendrickson Publishers Marketing, 2015

Brown, Driver, Briggs, and Gesenius. "Hebrew Lexicon entry for *Towb*". "*The Old Testament Hebrew Lexicon*". <http://www.studylight.org/lex/heb/view.cgi?number=2896>.

Girdlestone, Robert. *Synonyms of the Old Testament*. Grand Rapids, MI: Eerdmans, 1897/1973.

Gribbin, John, and Martin Rees. *Cosmic Coincidences*. New York, NY: Bantam Books, 1989.

Jamieson, Robert, A.R. Fausset and David Brown. *A Commentary Critical, Experimental, and Practical on the Old and New Testaments.* Grand Rapids, MI: Eerdmans, Ed. 1995. 1973.

Kaiser, Walter, The Literary Form of Genesis 1-11. "New Perspectives on the Old Testament" *Parallel Bible Commentary,* Nashville Tenn.: Thomas Nelson Publishers, 1994.

Keil, C. F. and F. Delitzsch. Volume I, *The Pentateuch. Biblical Commentary on the Old Testament.* Trans. by James Martin. Grand Rapids, MI: Eerdmans, no date.

Parallel Bible Commentary. Edward E. Hindson, Th.D, Woodrow Michael Kroll, Th.d., General Editors, Nashville: Thomas Nelson Publishers, 1994.

Philips, J. Robert Douglas, Ed. "Creation: The Biblical Doctrine" *The New Bible Dictionary*. Grand Rapids MI: Eerdmans, 1962.

Saint Augustine. *The City of God.* Trans. by Gerald G. Walsh, S.J.; Demetrius B. Zema, S.J.; Grace Monahan, O.S.U. Ed Vernon J. Bourke. New York, NY: Doubleday, 1958.

Wright, Richard T. *Biology Through the Eyes of Faith*. San Francisco CA: Harper Collins, 1989.

Chapter Six

THE MYSTERY OF HUMANITY

The creation of man is a far more complicated study than most of us imagine. In our study, this is the first time that we see the creation of a *compound being*, and as such it proves more difficult to understand. In addition, we have the problematic use of poetic language such as "God-breathed" and a reference to the internal counsel of God as He deliberates over His creation: "Let Us make man in Our image." As a result, the creation of man is seen as special and different from all other parts of God's creation, though all that He has made (*bara*) falls into the realm of the "miraculous." Although very rewarding, the study of man will be a complicated endeavor. Let us read the Hebrew Scriptures first:

Vs. 1:26 "God said, 'Let us <u>make</u> [asah S 6213] <u>man</u> [adam] with our image [tselem S 120] and likeness [demuwth S 1823]. Let him dominate the fish of the sea, the birds of the sky, the livestock animals, and all the earth and every land animal that walks the earth.'"

Vs. 1:27 "God [thus] created man with His image. In the image of God, He created him, male and female He creat-

ed them."

Vs. 2:7 "God formed man out of the dust of the ground, and breathed into his nostrils a breath of life. Man [thus] became a living creature."

Allowing the Bible to speak to us, we notice several things from the basic creation passages: (1) We are made in God's image, according to God's likeness; and (2) we are formed from the dirt of the ground.

God places His breath in a vessel made of the dust (Job 32:8; Prov. 20:27), of something from the earth (Job 4:19). Dust in the Bible usually refers to poverty and abasement, something of humble origins and common usage. Second, we notice that God's creative act makes a man a "living being". This special creation (apart from all other life forms) makes the creation of man as being composed of two elements: something common and coarse (clay, earth, dust) and something of divine and great potentiality (the breath of God).

Mankind is made up of two spheres: the sphere of the earth (ground) and the sphere of heaven (the breath of God). Man is connected to the created order by his body, and the divine and supernatural order by his immaterial spirit or soul. Man is a "compound being."

The compound nature of man has been the basis of much misunderstanding. If you see man only as purely natural or only of "dust," you will arrive at evolution. This theory says that man is a spontaneous production of the earth; therefore, he must be only earthly and material. This is an entirely atheistic doctrine. In a very true way, however, we can say that we are creatures, but we may not call ourselves "animals" or in any way "one" of many in the evolutionary chain of existence called "animal."

To see man only as "spiritual" as the New Age movement has, naturally leads us to pantheism, and we must find the "god" within us. The early fathers of the faith strenuously resisted both extremes. Professor Hodge further addresses this view which he calls Gnosticism. Gnosticism elevates the immaterial part of man as the only valid substance and denigrates the body, even going so far as to call it a "prison" for the soul. The mystery of mankind is that we are both spirit and matter. Without God's special revelation concerning our creation that we are made from both spheres—**and** that we are plural, the knowledge of ourselves will always be flawed.

The Scriptural account teaches us that the individual man consists of two distinct principles: a body with a soul; the one material and the other immaterial; the one corporeal and the other spiritual. These two principles are given in what the New Bible Dictionary calls, a "psychosomatic unity" (Douglas, 735). In other words, life from God is given in this unity and cannot stand or exist apart from one another. The Hebrews see man as an "animated body" in which "our distinctions between physical, intellectual and spiritual life do not exist."

6.1 THE SPHERE OF THE SPIRIT

Genesis 2:7 "God formed man out of the dust of the ground, and breathed into his nostrils a breath of life. Man [thus] became a living (hayyim S 2416) creature (nephesh S 5315)."

The first reference God makes about Himself is in conjunction with the creation of man. He uses the words "us" and "our." Both Jewish and Christian commentators say that this reflects the "plural of majesty." The sovereign of a nation speaks in the plural because he represents the authority of the state or the collective power of the people. God is not speaking in the plural of majesty as a king or president who represents the collective power of a people or even speaking for all the inhabitants of heaven. He is speaking in the collective power of the God-head, that is, in the three persons (powers) of the Trinity. Second, we notice that the means whereby man is made in God's image is through the impartation of the Spirit of God. This act makes the creation of Adam not only one of structural design (standing erect) but one of an interiority that is akin to God's being.

According to E.E. Ellis, Professor of New Testament Interpretation, the breath of God is God's Spirit, and it is synonymous with Life. Life, according to Dr. Ellis, carries with it the idea of "activity" or motion. Motion implies energy. He says, "Inherent in life [*hayyim S2416*] is the idea of activity. Life is that which 'moves' in contrast to the relaxed, dormant, or inert state of non-life" (Gen. 7:21-22; Ps. 69:34; Acts 17:28). In a sense, a river of running water is considered to be "living" in so far as it "moves" (Gen. 26:19 and Ps. 1:3). For this reason people are often tempted to describe rivers as having a "soul" or being "alive". This is a well-known practice among Hindus and Buddhists, as well as tribal religions, who worship these "living waters" and attribute divine powers to them. Jesus understood this concept when He referred to the "rivers of living water" as a picture of the activity of the Holy Spirit, the One who imparts divine life (John 4:14 and John 7:37-39). In the same vein, James 2:17-20 says, "Living faith" produces works or acts (has movement) while dead faith produces no activity; it is dead.

The breath constitutes Adam as (1) a special creation apart from other living creatures, and (2) unlike the animals he was infused (inspired) with God's own divine "life". Man alone is created by the "breath of God" which constitutes him as a "living soul". The word for "life" is *haya* while hayyim *(S 2416)* reflects a fuller dimension of life not shared with the other living creatures. Although the animals live and move, their life comes from the power of God's will alone. They do not have this fuller form of life called "*hayyim (S 2416)*."

In the Greek hayyim *S 2416* is always translated as *"Zoe"* (S 222) life or "resurrection-life" (both in the Septuagint and the Greek) or that which is immortal and eternal. In the Old Testament understanding as well as the New Testament, life properly belongs only to God (Ro. 5:21; Rev. 4:9; Jn. 5:26; 1 Tim. 6:16).

Thus, when God pronounced, "Let there be," He brought forth, out of the rich treasury of His mind, the fish, the birds, the beasts, and the cattle. God created forms that could walk and move and reproduce and even respond to one another. However, when God breathed the "breath of life" into Adam who became a "living soul," God topped His creation with life from "above". A "living soul" means an *immortal soul*, a soul that "liveth" as God does, forever. Thus the "crown" of God's creation does not necessarily refer to the making of man's body—though it is fearfully and wonderfully made—but to the infusion of God-type *hayyim* (S2416) life, an existence that far exceeds what all other forms of life possess. Keil and Delitzsch explain it as follows:

> *The breath of God became the soul of man; the soul of man, therefore, is nothing but the breath of God. The rest of the world exists through the word of God; [but] man [exists] through God's peculiar breath. This breath is the seal and pledge of our relation to God, of our godlike dignity; whereas the breath breathed into the animals is nothing but the common breath, the life-wind of nature, which is moving everywhere, and only appears in the animal fixed and bound into certain independence and individuality so that the animal soul is nothing but a nature-soul individualized into certain, though still material spirituality (Kiel and Delitzsch, I:79).*

Thus the life force or the vitality of man, the soul or spirit of man, was given by God and is immortal like the life of God Himself. This principally identifies man as being made after the image of God. His life (or soul) does not go down to the ground as the animals but returns to God for judgment or reward (Eccl.12:7). This is confirmed in Proverbs 20:27, "The spirit of a man is the lamp of the LORD, Searching all the inner depths of his heart." John 1:4 says, "In Him was life, and the life was the light of men."

It is astounding how vastly different we are from other creatures. While there is a commonality with other creatures we are vastly separate from them. The modern view that we are simply products of our biology will never be fully accepted without severe cognitive dissonance, insomuch that we are also creatures who ascribe meaning to our existence. A world without meaning is nihilism and ultimately unbearable. We are creatures who are aware of our surroundings, ourselves, and the complex interpersonal bonds that can exist between us. We are orators. We are communicators on a level vastly more sophisticated than animals. We are moral and rational in our basic constitution. We automatically ascribe justice to actions as well as recognize hierarchy in our relationships, whether personal or professional. These are boundaries that we respect. We are creatures that are driven by greater impulses than instincts. We are organizers, builders, creative and innovative, building cultures and beautifying our surroundings wherever we go. We find differentiation within ourselves, like the Godhead itself. We are divided in function into mind (reason), emotions (feelings), and will (the capacity for choice).

Furthermore, God has endowed us with the intrinsic abilities to know Him. There is a correlation between us. God made man in such a way as to reflect some of His perfections—perfect in knowledge, righteousness, holiness, and dominion over creatures; even perhaps the loving unity within the Godhead, that when properly united to God, we would reflect His glory in all the world. He made us like Himself. Wow, what a thought!

Even in a fallen state, God's image in man is still manifested. Men can do good things because in part they reflect these residual attributes of the original creation. The attribute of wisdom and knowledge produced in man are discernment, prudence, discretion, and wisdom. The attribute of goodness produces a desire to do good things to others, i.e., benevolent acts, kindness, graciousness, servanthood, and humility. The attribute of love produced in man is love, mercy, tenderness, compassion, hope, long-suffering, and patience. The attribute of righteousness produces in man a desire for holiness, justice, fairness, moderation, temperance, self-discipline, and self-control. God's truth, or reality, produces in man a need for honesty, faithfulness, trust, and loyalty. God's sovereignty produces in us a need for mutual respect, love, and a need for freedom, liberty, and independence. God's attribute of power produces in man a need for significance, purpose, direction, confidence, courage, and authority.

6.2 MALE AND FEMALE

Genesis 2:18 "God said, 'It is not good for man to be alone. I will make a **compatible helper** for him.'"

*Vs. 2:18 Vayomer Adonay Elohim lo-tov heyot ha'adam levado e'eseh-lo **ezer kenegdo**.*

The term "suitable" in Hebrew means *kenegdo* which is a three-part word: *ke* meaning like the *neged* meaning over and against or the opposite, and finally the o meaning him or man. This roughly approximates "man's corresponding opposition."

Now the term Adam (mankind) does not denote some kind of "earth creature" from which both man (is) and woman (*issa*) were formed. In other words, Adam was not split into (is) and (*issa*). Rather woman (*issa*) was derived from man (is). "Suitable" then means equality in substance since she was drawn from Adam, but it does not denote sameness, rather it denotes differentiation. Sameness would mean redundancy, not complimentary.

The anatomical differences in man and woman point to substantial psychological and physiological differences, and demonstrate that their roles in society were to be different even though both are equal in their humanity.

Adam, on seeing the woman, gave a prophetic utterance of the mystery of marriage when he said, "This is now bone of my bones and flesh of my flesh." He was saying effectively, "Wow, here is someone like me." Yet there were significant and obvious differences between them. His declaration reveals the truth about the mystery of marriage. Keil and Delitzsch say,

> "..marriage is the deepest corporeal and spiritual unity of man and woman... By the leaving of father and mother, which applies to the woman as well as to the man, the conjugal union is shown to be a spiritual oneness, a vital communion of heart as well as of body, in which it finds its consummation" (Keil and Delitzsch, 90-91).

Paul teaches mutual submission as seen in Ephesians 5 but at the same time teaches an element of "opposition" within this primordial dyad. If Eve is going to truly uphold Adam's glory, there must be an element of "opposition" (or otherness) in this relationship which must always remain one. This is why she is considered an *Ezer kenegdo*. The structural problem in homosexuality is that there is too much sameness. There is no tension in the relationship reflecting the whole portrait *icon* of God, it is too female, or too male in their relationship with one another. This principle is so strong that even in homosexual relationships there is still the internal need to break down the unit into these two opposites.

Now, why must there be two? Genesis 2:18 helps us understand how this works, "It is not good that the man should be alone; I will make him a helpmeet for him" (KJV). The word helper is *ezer (S 5828)*. There are many words for helper or help in the Bible, but the use of the word *Ezer* (noun) is reserved in the Bible for God nineteen times. It is used twice for Eve. When it is used for God it shows us that whenever God acts to help someone, always a weaker vessel or someone in need, the Scripture uses *Ezer,* and describes someone who has the strength or power to help someone else where that person lacks or is in need.

In this light, the fullest conception of being "a suitable helpmeet" then would be that Eve is to help Adam as God helps us in our weaknesses and needs. Nowhere do we find the term used of God as someone who is a slave or inferior, and much less to someone who is weak. On the contrary, Ezer (helper) refers to God (who is gracious and full of benevolent love) ready to assist and able to help. In the same way, women must "help" their husbands, working to maintain and establish his glory, i.e., helping him to glorify the LORD.

The Psalmist uses this term to describe God as one who gives help and also one who restrains. Psalm 46:1 and 54:4 use *Ezer* (the verb form) to demonstrate that the word has in itself no hint of inferiority. Indeed, the verses cited point to God as one who is strong enough to share His strength, and help another in a benevolent way. It is said of God in Exodus 18:4, "The God of my Father, [said he] was my help *[Ezer]*." In Deuteronomy 33:7 it is said, "Be thou a help *[Ezer]* to him from his enemies" (KJV). Abraham's servant is called an *"Eliezer"* meaning his servant and helper in all things urgent and important. *Eliezer* was tantamount to the chief steward of Abraham "who ruled over his whole household". Also, see Ebenezer which means "a stone of the help" which Samuel set up a few miles north of Jerusalem. It had reference to "the help" *[Ezer]* Israel received from God to defeat the Philistines (1 Sam 4:1,

5:1 and 7:12). The element of opposition is seen in the angel of the Lord who confronts Joshua on the road.

We can interpret the Genesis 2:18 passage as saying, "Eve is my help in times of trouble…she is my help in times of discouragement." Thus, Eve is fitted and gifted by God to fulfill this role in Adam's life as his Ezer. Note that Eve was to be an ezer to Adam even before sin had entered the world. Helping and caring and being there for others was God's original design and purpose for marriage.

There is a deeper meaning to Eve's creation. Eve was birthed out of the side of man. Eve is a helper not only by name but by creation. She was taken from her man and her goal is to be for her husband. She is to perform her tasks on earth in his service, for his good. He is her work. Together they may work on the cultural mandate but she must work for him in this greater work. Christ finds his being in God the Father, man finds it through Christ, and woman through man and children. This is by order of creation. Yet there is nowhere a hint of domination nor subjection in these orders. Other "Ezer(s)" in the Bible, like Sarah, Rebecca, Michal (David's wife), and Pilate's wife, what "help" did they give help to their husbands? What was the problem then?

6.3 "Let Them have Dominion…"

"And let them rule over the fish of the sea and the birds of the sky and the cattle and over all the earth, and over every creeping thing that creeps on the earth" (Genesis 1:28).

When God said, "Let them have dominion or let them rule" God underscored the fact that if man is to be like His Creator and exercise leadership or "taking dominion" would have to be in the mix. The calling and naming of the animals presuppose superiority over them because the greater always names the lesser. Adam became acquainted with the animals to learn their relationship to him, and by giving them names proves himself their lord. Furthermore, God does command him to name them, but by bringing the animals to him, God allows Adam to exercise his intellectual capacity that constitutes his superiority over the animal world.

The attributes God gave mankind are in effect "powers" that will enable Adam to work out his identity with royalty (Ps 8:5). Adam was to be the "lord of the earth" in God's name, he was to rule as His representative. He was to manifest God's glory in all that he said and did. In this way, the "divine image" in man would be manifest and God would be truly glorified. Therefore, man's royalty must be seen to be closely tied with dominion over the creation, which mankind is to exercise in God's name. With the faculty of mind and will man was enabled to subdue the earth, even though physically he proved to be one of the least of all the animals

Jamieson, Fausset and Brown say,

Already man rides master of the seas; he has subdued the stubborn soil; yoked the mighty energies of nature to his chariot; retained the lightning to whisper his messages along the air from state to state...probed the solid earth, and brought up its hidden wealth; analyzed her complex substances, and sealed up her elements where he can study their nature and their laws; measured her crystals, and used her coal...(Jamieson, Fausset and Brown, 1:20).

Adding space travel to his resume, it is true that man has indeed "subdued the earth" and beyond. It is not enough to have ideas or to pursue meaningless activities of pleasure (as the Islamic version of heaven has in the Qur'an), but man must have purpose and meaningful existence that yields results. This makes him like God who also has purpose and direction, who brings to pass the will of His desires. The ideal of lordship (dominion) can be seen in Dumbrell's excellent comment.

Man was to control his world, not primarily by immersing himself in the tasks of ordering it, but by recognizing that there was a system of priorities by which all of regulated life was to be controlled. If he were rightly related to his Creator, then he would rightly respond to creation (Dumbrell, 36).

6.4 THE ORIGIN OF SOULS

The age-old question of when life begins for Adam's descendants is really about at what point does the soul begin to exist and where does it come from? Three theories have been advanced.

1) **The preexistence of the soul.** Origen taught that the souls of men had a separate, conscious, personal existence in a previous state; that having sinned in that preexistent state, they are condemned to be born into this world in a state of sin in connection with a material body. According to Hodge, this view of Origen concerning the soul is the oriental view held by many in the East called the endless transmutation of the soul. "The Bible never speaks of a creation of men before Adam, or of any apostasy anterior to his fall, and it never refers the sinfulness of our present condition to any higher source beyond the sin of our first parents" (Hodge, 2:66-67).

2) **Traducianism.** The soul and the body are derived from the parents, commonly known as Traducianism. This theory denies that the soul is created; and affirms that it is produced by the law of generation, derived from the parents as is the body. According to this view the "whole man, soul, and body, is begotten" by the parents (Hodge 2:68-69). We disagree with Traducianism along several lines. (1) It implies that God is not active nor present in the generation of new souls after Adam. We feel this is a form of Deism, or certainly would lead to Deism. Traducianism holds that the soul is divisible and that every human being has received portions of Adam's soul which would support the popular notion of a "world-soul." We disagree with Traducianism in though the parents carry the seed of life, we understand Psalm 33:15 to

say that God "fashions their hearts individually" and Psalm 139:13 says that God "formed my inward parts," that He "covered me in my mother's womb" to mean that God is actively involved in the process both generating and sustaining life. Furthermore, we do not agree with the idea of the divisibility of the soul. Each man is given his own soul by God at conception which is not divisible. The ability to reproduce life from the cells of a body called "cloning" would not reproduce the same soul, but another body with the same DNA structure, yet having a different soul. What might be taken from the cellular structure would be biological life, not the soul of an individual, for the Scriptures say, "...each soul shall appear before Zion."

3) **Creationism.** This theory states that the soul of each man is immediately created at conception by God. Adherents to this view included the Greek and Latin church fathers. Later on, it was to include the Reformed churches and early Lutherans, who favored this view as believed to be in keeping with Scripture. However, later the Lutherans adopted Traducianism. Creationism is the view of Calvinists, including Hodge and Augustine (Hodge, 2:67, 70-71). We object to creationism for the following reasons. (1) It implies that God imputes sins or "corrupts" each soul as it is born and this would be tantamount to saying God creates evil including evil people. (2) It divides the unity/solidarity of Adam's progeny with Adam. (3) It makes sin only a legal or ethical issue (based upon propositional truth) rather than on a living active power that pervades man's being. (4) It unduly classifies the

race of mankind on the level of angels, each angel being a direct creation of God rather than a race that grows by propagation. Neither Cain, Abel, Seth, nor even Eve, were direct creations of God. Only Adam and Jesus fill this singular and distinct role in human history. (5) Furthermore, and probably the most cogent argument against this position is proposed by Professors Keil and Delitzsch who say that when God rested on the seventh day, it meant that He rested from His creative acts from the sixth day on. He now produces or creates by mediation through secondary causes and means. Man propagates and animals reproduce after their own kind. Adam, as the first man, was an immediate and direct creative act of God, as were all other works in creation before the seventh day.

4) **Simultaneous Generation.** Our view is that the soul is the animating principle of human life as follows: In looking at Genesis 1:11 we see that it says the "seed is in the fruit," each according to its "kind." When that verse is taken (comparing spiritual things with spiritual things) with 1 Corinthians 15:38-39, "But God gives it a body as He pleases, and to each seed its own body. All flesh is not the same flesh, but there is one kind of flesh of men, another flesh of animals, another of fish, and another of birds. There are also celestial bodies, and terrestrial bodies." We understand this to mean that mankind also reproduces after his own kind. The "seed of life" is resident within man as well. Genesis 5:1-3 is written in such a way that we are to understand that Seth was

born in the image of Adam as this is contrasted with Adam who was made in the image of God.

We know from biology that cell division (*mitosis*) is the mysterious impulse in the development of life. How and what makes cell division occur has never been fully understood. Medical science affirms that the egg is an inert mass made up of dense protein. The egg itself contains no activity, but lies dormant and waiting to be "quickened" (the idea is 'enlivened'), and if not quickened, then it is expelled. When it is expelled, there is no loss of human life, only loss of human potential for life.

On the other hand, the "male sperm" is full of life, i.e., "activity," and this life or energy is the "seed" that carries the life force. At penetration of the egg, it is medically said to "respire" as if the egg takes a deep breath. In slow-motion photography, you can see the egg as it is penetrated by the sperm, it takes a breath, "It breathes in" for the very first time. It immediately begins to divide and at this point has been quickened and is very much a person. Thus, the first breath that a new soul takes is not at birth (at delivery) but at conception, or at the moment of quickening wherein a human being has been created. So we say that the seed (or the sperm) is the agent which carries both the animating and tainted principle of life, as well as the components (chromosomes) that complete the body. The material body now serves to tabernacle the "life-vitality" of the human being and thus the soul is formed. We say that the impetus for movement, or the "energy" or the "life-vitality" in the process of *mitosis*, is the original life or breath that God placed within the human seed to create a human soul.

6.5 THE SOUL'S CORRUPTION

In light of the above, how then, is sin transmitted from generation to generation? What began with such a noble beginning, its perfect state has taken a dramatic turn. What is our solidarity with Adam? Following our thinking so far, we see that the corrupt life-vitality is passed through the male seed to the inert mass of protein (the ovum) that the woman carries that forms the body.

In other words, the gift of life, originally given by God, has been corrupted. The apostle Peter underscores this interpretation when he says, "Since you have purified your souls in obeying the truth through the Spirit...having been born again, not of corruptible seed but of incorruptible, through the word of God which lives and abides forever" (1 Peter 1:22-23). The Apostle Paul confirms this also when he says in 1 Corinthians 15:42, "The body is sown in corruption, it is raised in incorruption." In verse 53 Paul says, "For this corruptible must put on incorruption, and this mortal must put on immortality" (See also John 3:3-6; 2 Cor.. 5:17 and Jas. 1:18).

With this understanding, and by looking at the particulars of the birth of Jesus, we find even greater clarity. For example, in Jesus' birth the Holy Spirit interrupted the normal sequence of events, i.e., Joseph's seed is substituted with a new seed by the

Holy Spirit, thereby quickening the egg of Mary with a new "breath" of God. Thus Jesus was the only other direct creation after the first man Adam. The soul of Jesus was a perfectly new and untainted creation, untainted by the corrupted seed of fallen man. This is what's meant by the virgin birth of Jesus. This also is why Paul refers to Jesus as the Second Adam (See 1 Cor. 15:45 and Luke 1:35).

Some have imputed sinlessness on Mary to accomplish the same result. However, if they understood that Mary's egg, like all other female eggs, was inert only having the potential for life, then a new and direct breath by God by His Spirit would make the birth of Jesus fully sinless. This also argues against the position that sin resides in the body. Rather, it resides (biblically speaking) in the seed of man. Therefore, we understand and can say that sin is not imputed to new souls when they are conceived; rather, new souls are conceived in sin, therefore are sinful due to the corrupted seed of man at conception. The corruptible seed refers to Adam's seed passed on to all of humanity. The incorruptible seed, however, refers to the new birth from above available to all, which is the second work of the Spirit toward humanity and the emblem of God's love for all mankind (1 Cor. 15:47,49).

The New Bible Dictionary beautifully states that man's true-life originates and is grounded in Jesus Christ, who "became a life-giving spirit" (1 Cor. 15:20) (Douglas, 737). When Jesus "blows" or actually "breathes" upon men it is the regeneration of their souls (See John 20:22 and John 3:3-5). A new seed has been given. A fresh soul has been granted, renewed through the crucifixion of Christ.

Discussion Questions

1. What are the pitfalls of not understanding the compound nature of man?

2. In what way can we agree with evolutionists and new-agers on the nature of man?

3. When we say that man is the crown of creation, we often think this refers only to the "image of God" in man, but what other feature makes him far above all other creatures?

4. According to this course, the seed of Mary was pure because of what? What does the "New Adam" refer to?

5. To which theory of generation do you hold?

Bibliography

Douglas, Robert, Ed. *New Bible Dictionary.* Grand Rapids, MI: Eerdmans, 1962.

W.J. Dumbrell, Covenant and Creation, *A Theology of the Old Testament Covenants.* Grand Rapids: Baker Book House, 1984

Elwell, Walter A. *An Evangelical Dictionary of Biblical Theology.* Grand Rapids: Baker Book House, 1996

Hodge, Charles. *Systematic Theology.* 3 Vols. New York: Scribner And Sons, 1989.

International Standard Bible Encyclopedia. Electronic Database: Biblesoft, 1996.

Jamieson, Robert, A.R. Fausset, and David Brown. *A Commentary Critical, Experimental, and Practical on the Old and New Testaments.* Grand Rapids: Wm. B. Eerdmans, 1995.

Keil, C.F. and F. Delitzsch. Trans. by James Martin. *The Pentateuch. Biblical Commentary on the Old Testament..* Grand Rapids: Wm. B. Eerdmans, 1877

Chapter Seven

THE MYSTERY OF THE SABBATH REST

Thus the heavens and the earth were completed, and all their hosts were. By the seventh day, God completed His work which He had done, and He rested on the seventh day from all His work that He had done. Then God blessed the seventh day and sanctified it because in it He rested from all His work which God had created and made(Genesis 2:1-3 NASB).

Genesis 2:1-3 is a summary statement reflecting the totality of creation—the things of heaven (the heaven of heavens, the angels) and the things of earth (animals, plants, and man). God can cease His work because He had brought everything up to His ideal for it. Creation had reached its *telios (S5046-7)* moment, the end for which it was created—to support life and loving relationships in gracious stability. He then could bless it, hallow it, and call it good. It is called "good" insofar as it (1) perfectly fulfills the purpose for which it was created and (2) because in all its ways it glorifies the Creator. So God enters into His rest, in the "...rest of His all-sufficient eternal Being, from which He had come forth, as it were, in the creation of a world distinct from His own essence" (Kiel and Delitzsch, 1:68). God's ceasing to create is called "resting" or a "refreshing" (Ex. 31:17). This is a different function from the "governance of the world" which He continues to do today as Jesus indicated, "My Father is always working" (John 5:17). In Genesis 2:2, it meant that He ceased from His labors of creating things "out of nothing". The governing of the world is not his work in the sense of *"bara"*—a production of extreme energy and power—in which all the powers of the God-head were involved. His "work" has now become His pleasure in which "all spiritual powers stream forth from Him as a blessing." It is helpful to use the analogy here of a garden. The initial work of making a garden is a backbreaking effort. There is the breaking up of the ground, the rooting out of rocks and weeds, and the removal of extra soil to make room for new life. Once the garden is sown and growth begins, the gardener's true pleasure has begun. In the same way, God now enjoys the fruits of His initial works and acts like a husbandman.

7:1 THE WORK OF MEDIATION BEGINS

"He rested (*Shabat*—#H7673) on the seventh day from all "His work (*Malakah*—#H4399) which He had done."

On the seventh day of creation, which is still open, God moves from His role of Creator to one of preserving life, "In whom we move and live and have our being" (Acts 17). When God rested from His *"bara"* works, He decreed that life should primarily be continued through the process of *mediation*. He mediates through the principle of the seed which He has designed, each seed with its own body. When the seventh day closes, God will once again create in His *"bara" (S 1254)* sense.

He will make a renewed heaven and a new earth, and a new Jerusalem (Isaiah 65:17-18; 2 Peter 3:13; Revelation 21:1-2), and resurrect the dead unto immortality (1 Corinthians 15:52-56).

In this open day, however, He uses means to perpetuate life. Mediation begins with the visible world and moves to the invisible one—the physical realm and continues to the spiritual realm. The pattern is the same in both. In the physical world, He fixes the laws of the universe, of planets, seas, and seasons that will establish the world in the assurance of its continuance until He calls an end to its existence. In speaking to Job in verse 38:33, God asks Job, "Do you know the *ordinances* of the heavens, or fix their rule over the earth?"

There is a three-fold purpose for establishing the world through these natural fixed laws as an outworking of God's covenant with us.

First, "Man as a creature" needs order and stability for his psychic integrity. Perception is fragile and must be preserved in a state of equilibrium. The world must not be perceived as threatening, hostile, or unpredictable for mankind to flourish. Creation cannot be in a state of constant change. Both the mind and reproduction of the species demand constancy and predictability. This need for stability is one of the reasons that miracles are so mind-boggling. The mind has no "cubby hole" for its existence. It is beyond man's reasoning powers. Furthermore, man is a being that categorizes and *establishes meaning or interprets meaning* through a fixed universe. He is a builder and a beautifier. In constant change, meaning cannot be ascribed other than "chaos."

Second, man was given the commandment to "subdue the earth and take dominion." The earth was given to Adam as a trust in which Adam was to subdue the earth and bring it under his dominion. He cannot be about the business of building and subduing the earth if suddenly a new mountain range appears that had not been there yesterday. The world must come under his power if he is to be a true regent. In the book *Perelandra,* by CS Lewis, the ground was always moving beneath the feet of its inhabitants. There is a scene in which the female character is taken away by one such movement of earth. It is only the earthling that is distraught by this unpredictable turn of events. "Where are you going?" he asks as she drifts away from him. "Does it matter? Why must you humans always know where you are going?" she asks. Going doesn't mean anything to her, but it does to a man. "Being lost" or long-term disorientation is fertile ground for a mental breakdown and is often a symptom of psychotic behavior. In *Perelandra* there were few if any constants—a world in which all meaning is in flux.

Third, to establish in the mind of man the faithfulness and loving-kindness of God the Father. There must be in the mind of man a "plausibility structure" for believing in the existence of a "good God." For this reason, God endows the world with an abundance of flavors, sounds, textures, experiences, flora, and fauna all seen in the heavens, the earth, and the seas. The world was created to display the evidence of a majestic and yet *maternal* Being who delights in satisfying the heart of man but also keeping him safe. For the above reasons, God works through three mediating principles that are seen throughout the Bible and are intricately woven together: Promise, Covenant, and Prayer. All of our encounters with God are mediated through Promise, Covenant, and Prayer.

To Noah, he said, "Now behold I Myself do establish My covenant with you, and with your descendants after you; and with every living creature that is with you, the birds, the cattle, and every beast of the earth with you; of all that comes out of the ark, even every beast of the earth. Never again will I curse the ground because of humans, even though every inclination of the human heart is evil from childhood. And never again will I destroy all living creatures, as I have done. ...As long as the earth endures, seedtime and harvest, cold and heat, summer and winter, day and night will never cease. Whenever the rainbow appears in the clouds, I will see it and remember the everlasting covenant between God and all living creatures of every kind on the earth" (Genesis 8:21-9:16).

The continuity of the rainbow became a sign of the faithfulness of God and that life will go on. The promise to never again destroy was given in a covenantal form.

A covenant is an agreement between two people and involves commitments from both parties, Covenant was the most solemn and most indissoluble conceivable (Precepts). The concept of a covenant between God and His people is one of the central themes of the Bible. Covenants always include a cutting or a shedding of blood and sanctions if the parties do not keep the covenant. Other biblical covenants include those made to Abraham, Moses, David, and in Christ Jesus (The New Covenant).

Prayer is the language of the covenant. He does nothing apart from the prayer of His people. Apart from the forensic issue of free will, He chooses to work through the (mediated) words and requests of His people. He seldom works without this intervention on their part. In the judgment on Sodom and Gomorrah, God is set on destroying this city because of the outcry over its wickedness. Then He says to Himself, "Shall I hide from Abraham what I am about to do?" He does this for two reasons (1) He had a covenant with Abraham to do a task that would involve the world and (2) He works through delegated leadership. He does not undermine the authority that He had invested in Abraham or Adam as the head of all creation. Man is the head of creation, all things about life on earth, including people, will be mediated through the people of God. God will not act independently of His agents, beginning with the apostles and prophets and then His wider body. Prayer is one of the principal means of accomplishing the will of God on earth. For this reason, he raises entire congregations of people to do nothing but pray so that their inspired prayers will be answered by His need. If he needs to rescue a drowning child, he will first burden a believer with this need and supply the need. God's rest then becomes our "burden." We help continue the ongoing work of redemption and recreation.

Jesus was the means whereby God the Father reconciled the world to Himself (John 3:16). Jesus was the author or mediator of the whole created order (John 1:1). Christ is the mediator between God and man, and salvation was how we are reunited with the Father and filled by the Holy Spirit. Jesus baptizes us through the gift of the Spirit who is the means of the sanctifying love of God within us. The Holy Spirit was the sign of this New Covenant. Jesus and the Father are mediated through the love of God which is the Spirit.

For the spiritual man or woman, rest should reflect our life in God and that we have rested from our "own fleshly" works and we delight in doing the will of God. We know that God will take care of us and that He will provide for us all our needs. It is a glorious state of being, like Jesus who sat down at the right hand of God when His work was finished. In this sense, God as Creator also rested.

7.5 TO BLESS (BARAK—#H1288)

In part, we have already seen a glimmer of this idea in the word "rest." Now we see a fuller development in the word, *to bless*. The activity of God so far has been: He ceases, He rests and He blesses. Both words for bless (*Barak S 1288* and *brakah, S 1293*) refer to a form of benediction in which the greater bestows something on the lesser, a benefit, a favor, peace, or a gift. It is the opposite of "to curse". In its fullest meaning, it means that God "breathes" His favor, His presence upon a certain time, article, event, or person. To bless means to be declared "acceptable" in His sight. Of course, we know that God's breath is the presence of His Spirit upon us and in us. It was not only the seventh day that was made holy, but on the 6th day, after he had created man and woman He blessed them and said, "Be fruitful and multiply, and fill the earth and subdue it...." He infused them with power, with virtue, with an apostolic mandate to rule over the earth in these few verses.

"The divine act of blessing," says the *Jewish Virtual Library*, "was a real communication of powers of salvation, grace, and peace; and sanctifying was not merely declaring holy but communicating or imparting the attribute of holy" (Kiel and Delitzsch 1:69). It signified that the land was holy, undefiled and good—able to be inhabited and visited by God without restraint (unlike later when the land became polluted). It was pleasant to man and pleasurable to God, open to God's presence. Israel was to keep the living relationship with God so that the land and its inhabitants would remain pure so that God could "walk among us."

A secondary meaning of the word " blessed" is the idea that God breathes His life upon creation. It is an anointing of sorts in which we get the idea of empowerment. When we bless things or people in a real way we are infusing them with life-giving grace from above.

In this sanctifying impartation, there are all the elements of a covenant. God will provide and take care of His creation. It is His commitment to us. He infuses a part of Himself into the creation, His goodness, His oversight, and protection.

Discussion Questions

1. Please explain the apparent contradiction of Genesis 5:1 "He rested [*Shabat*—S 7673]S 4399 on the seventh day from all His work [*Malakah*—S 4399] which He had done" and "My Father is always working?" (John 5:17)

2. God uses *means* to perpetuate life. Mediation begins with the visible world and moves to the invisible one—the physical realm and continues to the spiritual realm. How is prayer a means to an end? Does this change your view of prayer?

3. One of the overarching themes in the Bible is the theme of wilderness and journey. How does the word "rest" speak to this journey?

4. Both words for blessing *barak*—Strongs #1288 and *brakah*, Strongs #1293 refer to a form of benediction in which the greater bestows something on the lesser, a benefit, a favor, peace, or a gift. Expand on the theme of "and He blessed creation and called it good."

5. When we say, "God bless you!" to someone, what are we asking God to do?

Bibliography

Jewish Virtual Library.org/jsource/Judaism/shabbat1.html

Keil, C.F. and F. Delitzsch. Trans. by James Martin. *The Pentateuch. Biblical Commentary on the Old Testament.* Grand Rapids: Wm. B. Eerdmans, no date.

Precepts: http://www.preceptaustin.org/covenant_in_the_bible.htm

Chapter Eight

The Mystery of Paradise

Eden was a special place designed by God, especially for Adam and Eve. It was to serve three main functions — to give man purpose, to provide for his physical needs, and to show the abundance of God's love toward them. This special place because of its lush green beauty and fruitfulness is called a garden (Gen. 2:8,15; Ezek. 36:33-37). It is sometimes called the "Vineyard of the Lord" and is seen as the epitome of God's goodness towards man.

Used symbolically, the vineyard was the emblem of prosperity and peace among the ancient Hebrews, encapsulated in the term shalom, i.e., well-being. A state in which nothing was broken, nothing was missing—a state of perfection and wholeness. From this perspective we can see that the whole earth was to be filled with peace and tranquility, the evidence of God's presence (Hab. 2:14). From Isaiah 51:3-4 we see that the garden was a place of joy, gladness, thanksgiving and that the "voice of melody" could always be heard.

Some imagine that Adam was a mere brute in his original state and had to slowly come or evolve into his dignity as a person; perhaps living in caves and fighting dinosaurs! Others imagine that Adam had wondrous powers, using more of his brain power than man uses today—a sort of superhero. Still, others imagine Adam to be simple, naive, and innocent, unprepared to make the judgments that God will ask him to make. However, we want the Bible, not our imaginations, to explain to us the mysteries of Paradise. To understand both the state of life and the quality of life in the garden of the Lord, we need to investigate two key passages in the New Testament in which we see the original constitution of man.

8.1 THE GOODNESS OF ADAM

The apostle Paul says in Colossians 3:10, to "...put on the new man, who is renewed in knowledge, according to the image of Him who created him...." It's critical to unpack this loaded verse. When the apostle Paul refers to the "new man" he is referring to the "recreated" man; the man who has been "born from above" through the agency of the Holy Spirit. God recreates him as he once created the first man after "the image and likeness of God." Remember that only Adam was made "in the image of God." Cain and Abel were born after the fall, and in the "image of Adam" (Gen. 5:1) The fractured self that Adam found in himself, after his disobedience, passed on to his sons.

So now regeneration is the act and process of restoring to us that which was lost: converting us to the original image of God, in what theologians call the "essential image of God," His moral perfection. That process involved being "renewed in knowledge." This is not mere intellectual knowledge, for Adam did not lose his rational faculties when he sinned, but he lost the essence of what it meant to be made in the image and likeness of God—he lost the "knowledge" that is a full, accurate, living and practical experiential knowledge of God and as a result, his intellect was darkened.

Professor Hodge says that this is not to say that the new man was recreated "in knowledge, much less by knowledge, but unto knowledge, so that he knows. Knowledge is the effect of the renovation spoken of" (Hodge, 2:99-100). This verse tells us that original man possessed such knowledge, true knowledge, the kind that God Himself possesses, i.e., truth. Hodge, in that same passage, states that such knowledge is eternal life, and includes what in Ephesians 4:24 is expressed as "righteousness and holiness." The loss of knowledge also meant the loss of man's moral purity, his original righteousness. Rather than become "like God" as Satan had predicted, he lost his likeness to God in its fullness.

This passage reveals "the original likeness to God in which man was created, and to which the believer is restored," (in Christ) is restored "after the image of Him who created him."

In this passage, Paul says, "...Put on the new man, which after God is created in righteousness and true holiness". In other words, the new man we are to put on is "after God" consisting of "righteousness and holiness." This is the effect of what it means to "walk in the truth" (See Micah 6:8; Titus 1:8; Heb. 12:23; Rev. 15:3).

These two passages make it very clear that righteousness, knowledge, and holiness were God's original gifts to man. The apostle Paul says, "But the natural man does not receive the things of the Spirit of God, for they are foolishness to him; nor can he know them" (1 Cor. 2:14). The assertion is that Adam's mind, as he came from the hands of his Maker, was imbued with spiritual and divine knowledge. This knowledge does not refer to knowledge of the material world but to the knowledge of God and spiritual knowledge, that man has subsequently lost. (See 1 Cor. 2:12)

Furthermore, the character of the new man is also described in Colossians 3:12 as "...the elect of God, holy and beloved, put on tender mercies, kindness, humility, meekness, long-suffering; bearing with one another, and forgiving one another... Above all these things, put on love which is the bond of perfection." Thus, we can conclude that Adam and Eve lived in "the truth" and this manifested a character of moral purity and grace, not as some dumb brute. Adam's state of being is what theologians call the "original state of righteousness and blessedness," not totally unlike what Jesus had, who in His humanity also possessed. Adam, before he fell, must have remarkably resembled Jesus in his humanity.

Righteousness in Adam produced a life of perfect harmony. There was harmony between God and man, and this harmony extended and affected all other parts of creation. There was harmony between Adam and Eve, between Adam and the environment, and finally between Adam and himself. In this state,

Adam's "reason was subject to God, his will was subject to his reason, and his affections and appetites were subject to his will..." (Hodge, 2:99). In this state, Adam's body was in perfect submission to his affections (1 Cor. 6:19) which longed after the will and Word of God as described throughout Psalm 119. Thus, Adam and Eve reflected the self-control and sweetness of spirit which comes from being made in the image of God. No rebellion or disproportion between them needed to be balanced having the fruits of the Spirit. Finally, Adam experienced the perfect harmony with God that comes from being pure and righteous. He had been made for just such fellowship to which he employed knowledge and love. In short, Adam was holy like God is holy. There was no cognitive dissonance between what he believed in his mind and how he acted in his body. His body obeyed his mind in all matters.

Every aspect of man's life was supreme and yet also holy from the moment of creation. All of life was pervaded and inspired by divine insights and everything was valued as having come from the hand of God. In this state of moral purity and joy, Adam was free to be vulnerable, he was able to display and live his humanity to the full, and as such he could easily double his joy. Not having to pretend, control, succeed, or hide, he could afford to be creative, inventive, and communicative with Eve. It was similar to children who play freely without the pain of self-consciousness (1 Cor. 10:24). Unlike children, they had a fully developed awareness of God and themselves. For to know God is to know oneself. The more we know Him, the more we know and understand ourselves.

Eve also experienced great satisfaction and fulfillment in the garden for she was loved without guile and reservation. Her joy was truly doubled as she shared with her husband the management of the world. They were free and fully able to discover God's great world together. So life in Paradise was not a mindless existence. God had given Adam and Eve their royal duties as representatives of God over all of God's beautiful creations on earth. The daily challenges were met with a ready supply of divine inspiration, revelation, wisdom, and power.

God begins by giving three institutions. *Institution*, as defined by Britannia World Language Dictionary, means that which is "instituted or established, an established order, principle, law for usage as an element of organized society or civilization, [like] the institution of chivalry." In other words, these institutions are the bedrock laws of civilization or elemental rudimentary instructions for the organization of human society. These were not simple desires that God expressed, but had long-reaching and profound implications for all of human life.

8.2 STEWARDSHIP/WORK

God begins by introducing the institution of work or a more biblical concept of "stewardship." In Adam's pursuit to exercise his royal prerogative as God's representative, Adam was to till the earth and to name the animals (Dan. 2:37-38; Jer. 27:6). A steward is a person entrusted with the management of estates or affairs not his own. He was to develop the natural resources at his disposal. His work in this pursuit is considered a position of trust. In the Old Testament, a steward is a man who is over a house that belongs to someone else. In Adam's case, the "house" was the creation itself that belonged to God (1 Cor. 4:1-2; Titus 1:7; 1 Pt. 4:10). Work was not the result of the fall, for both mental and manual labor is given as a delegated responsibility before the fall. We could say that up to this point, God has been doing the work of tending the garden, but now He shares the responsibility with His image-bearers. In this way, we become co-laborers with God in maintaining and governing the world for His glory. The legal authority to rule over this "house" came from God Himself. We must see work as God's divine gift to man. It gives man purpose, the optima challenge for an intellectual creation. Truly we are to be stewards of the earth so that God's glory would be fully displayed and thereby undoing the works of the devil.

8.3 MARRIAGE

The second institution God introduced in the garden was marriage. The purpose of which is to share life and love with another and to teach one to live for someone other than himself. This benevolent and committed context was meant to bring children into the world and multiply humanity throughout the earth. The ensuing bond was to be culturally and legally protected to ensure that the family would flourish. Marriage and the begetting of children were God's way of expressing harmony, love, and joy on earth as seen in the Godhead.

8.4 LAW

The third institution was that of law. The law was a simple and beautiful declaration resting in God's love for mankind. God simply mandated, "...Of the tree of the knowledge of good and evil you shall not eat..." (Gen. 2:17). This limitation on their freedom was established so that man could recognize God's divine right to rule over him. The institution of law provided mankind with the means to exercise his free will on behalf of God's will.

With these three institutions in place, essentially the context was set for Adam and Eve to live happy fulfilled lives. All of creation had been posed for this one single event, the coming of man and the enjoyment of his new habitat in fellowship with God his Creator. The only prohibition (law) in the garden was the prohibition to eat of one particular tree, in which God warned man, "...for in the day that you eat of it you shall surely die" (Gen. 2:17).

8.5 THE FREEDOM OF ADAM

In Lesson Two we mentioned the necessity of Adam needing to be a free moral agent. This was due to Adam being made in God's image. We know that God is free. God is without any hindrances to be Himself in the fullest way. God's desire is for man to be like Him in that way also, not in an absolute way, but relative to God. This is the clearest definition of what it means to be a "person." Freedom is universally important to all men everywhere because we are made in God's image.

Free Will

In psychological terms, we can understand that freedom is composed of reason and the power of self-determination.

> "Whenever reason and self-determination [the will] are combined and operate in an agent, he or she is said to be free. For instance, maniacs have a will or self-determination but are irrational, hence they are not free. In brutes there is spontaneity but no reason, therefore, they are not free" (Hodge, 2:286).

Therefore, when reason and the active and spontaneous power of the will exist in combination to fulfill an individual's thoughts and desires, we say that such a person is free. For we know that reason without power can accomplish nothing, while power without reason is irrational and chaotic.

John Calvin in his *Institutes* organizes these truths as follows:

> *The human soul consists of two faculties, understanding [reason] and will [self-determination]. Let the office of understanding be to distinguish between objects, as each seems worthy of approval or disapproval; while that of the will, [is] to choose and follow what the understanding pronounces "good" and to reject and flee what it disapproves....the understanding is, as it were, the leader and the governor of the soul; and that the will is always mindful of the bidding of the understanding, and...awaits the judgment... Therefore God provided man's soul with a*

mind, by which to distinguish good from evil, right from wrong; and, with the light of reason...what should be followed from what should be avoided... To this, he [God] joined the will, [under whose control is choice] (Calvin, 1:194-5).

Views (thoughts, as well as beliefs) or feelings (motives, desires) condition the will, the choice. Drs. Hodge and Fuller, as well as Augustine and Calvin, concur that what people understand to be satisfying, either the craving of nature or the spirit, they label as good; and what is perceived to be evil they decide against. What they perceive to be good forms (advises) or conditions the will. They will, then, be positioned between conflicting motives. It can choose for the nature of the self, the "old man," or it can choose for the recreated self in the image of God.

The term "free will" simply means mankind has both the cognitive ability to perceive truth *and* the self-determination to choose. In layman's terms, it means that as human beings we have the knowledge to perceive whether something is good or bad, and we have the power and ability (freedom) to decide for or against a given matter. In other words, we are free to make choices. The problem with fallen man is that He does not have the will to live according to the truth, even though he may very well want to—a sort of "the spirit is willing but the flesh is weak."

Yet in a very real sense, man is free to do so if he had the power to do what he wanted to do. As St. Paul cried out, "I don't understand myself, for I want to do what is right, but I don't do it. Instead, I do what I hate." Romans 7:15 and Galatians 5:17 say, "For the sinful natures desires what is contrary to the Spirit, and the Spirit what is contrary to the sinful nature. The conflict with each other so that you do not do what you want." Paul goes on to say, "Oh wretched man. Who will deliver me from this body of death?" The answer is Jesus Christ our Lord, "...For the law of the Spirit of life set me free from the law of sin and death, ...for He condemned sin in sinful man. For those who live according to the sinful nature have their minds set on what that nature desires, but those who live by the Spirit have their minds set on what the Spirit desires" (Romans 7-8 NIV).

We are often presented with a choice, we can choose for our lower natures; i.e., self, flesh, the world, or to choose against ourselves (against our lower nature) which is to glorify God and to believe His interpretation of the facts. It is the way of the Cross, for often, the self is emotionally and intellectually committed to the opposite position of God's Word. The Bible says that if we reap to the flesh, we will sow destruction, but if we sow to the Spirit we will reap eternal life. Thinking on the things of the Spirit strengthens the will to desire the good, meditating on the things of the flesh only weakens the will, *and sooner or later, the body will act out by the desires of the diminished will.*

Returning to Adam, he was endowed with free will, by which if he had chosen to believe and obey God's Word he would have obtained his reward.

8.6 IMMORTALITY VS. ETERNAL LIFE

Adam's privileged role and position in the garden of the Lord indicate that Adam was morally pure and blameless before God. In this sense, we can say that Adam was holy because he was made "good" at his initial creation. Because Adam walked with God, we can say that Adam's goodness was synonymous with his holiness. However, we must understand that this "goodness" or "holiness" was not an attribute of Adam, as was his intelligence, his feelings, and his will, but only by his initial creation. In other words, holiness is an attribute of God, without it, God could not be God. Similarly, reason, emotion, and will are attributes of man, without which man could not be a man. Goodness or holiness was not an attribute of Adam's nature nor was it something of his own doing; rather, it was a state in which he lived by divine grace. Therefore, his possession of holiness remained as long as he was properly related to God. *This is to say that Adam, though morally pure, was still subject to temptation and therefore vulnerable to sin, and therefore—vulnerable to death.* Although Adam enjoyed an unparalleled state of blessedness, he nonetheless was not immune to sin (Vos, 31). Adams' goodness as well as his unlimited fellowship with God was, therefore, subject to loss.

Adam's vulnerability to temptation was in part due to his freedom to obey or disobey God. Adam's vulnerability to death was due in its totality to his vulnerability to sin. We must see that death's entrance into human life could only come through sin. There is no biological or spiritual death apart from sin (Rom

5:12,17; 6:23; 1 Cor. 15:21; James 1:15). We exclaim, "I thought Adam's soul was immortal?" So let us examine biblical and philosophical immortality.

Philosophical vs. Biblical Immortality

Immortality in the philosophical sense expresses the idea of the persistence of the soul, which even when the body is dissolved still retains its identity and its existence. In this sense, every human being under all circumstances is immortal. So too were our first parents before and after the fall (Hodge, 3:299).

Immortality in the biblical sense is radically different. Biblically speaking, immortality is that state of man in which he has nothing in himself which would cause death. It is quite possible to say that the existence of death hangs over man (Ps 23:4) because man is free to exercise his will toward sin. This was also true of Adam before he disobeyed His Maker and Creator.

Dr. Fuller gives a wonderful analogy that will help us understand this state: Though we presently do not have cancer, we nonetheless are not immune from getting it. Likewise, though Adam was made morally pure, he was not immune to sin. His state of blessedness was subject to loss.

Thus, biblical or theological immortality (or eternal life) is that state of man in which he has been made immune to death because he has been made immune to sin. This is the state which He desires us to achieve—a state in which man is no longer vulnerable to sin, therefore, no longer subject to death. The indwelling presence of God is the incorruptible seed that upon believing in Christ "keeps us" or "seals us" unto the day of redemption and glorification (Eph... 1:13-14; 2 Cor. 1:22). Scriptures say,

> *But those who are counted worthy to attain that age, and the resurrection from the dead, neither marry nor are given in marriage; nor can they die anymore, for they are equal to the angels and are sons of God, being sons of the resurrection (Luke 20:35-36; cf John 6:47-51 and 11:26).*

Two things are important in this verse. First, men who are counted worthy at the end of the age can no longer die. Why is it that they can no longer die? Sin is the only way into death, it must mean that those believers can no longer sin. Second, it means that we have been made equal to the angels where prior we were made a "little lower" than they are. In what way? "Now it is God who has made us for this very purpose..." (2 Cor. 5:5, NIV). What purpose? To be clothed with the blessed immortality of eternal life not just the persistence of the soul after death. Eternal life becomes his or her possession when this occurs. Therefore, when God offers us eternal life, He offers us everlasting life, a higher state of perfection (glorification) than Adam had before the fall.

Hence, the philosophical concept of immortality falls devastatingly short of *eternal life.* It is not mere immortality but a life in which there is no threat to its existence, it is not subject to loss! It means unlimited access to God throughout eternity wherein is the fullness of joy. Because we are immortal shall it be spent with God in righteousness or shall it be spent in eternal darkness separated from Him? True immortality is the possession of God, first of all, who has it by nature (1 Tim 6:16); and second, it is the possession of the glorified Christ who has it by His obedience (Eph. 4:10); and third, it is the possession of the regenerated people of God who have it by virtue of the Holy Spirit

8.7 ADAM'S CONFIRMATION (ESTABLISHED)

Adam's goodness and fellowship with God before the fall were unconfirmed or untested goodness. God had indeed given Adam eternal existence, but besides that, He also wanted to give Adam eternal life. God wanted to move Adam from a state of unconfirmed goodness to one of confirmed goodness. "Man had been created perfectly good in a moral sense. Yet there was a sense in which he could be raised to a still higher level of perfection" (Vos, 31). The advance would mean going to a state in which he could no longer lose his state of blessedness. It would mean a state of unchangeableness in what he already possessed. The potential for such a conversion and goal is seen by the "tree of life" which was placed in the center of the garden (representing God's perfect and ultimate will for mankind).

Adam had not yet eaten of the tree of life—its mysterious properties had not been disclosed to him. Scriptures lead us to this conclusion for the following reasons: (1) The nature of being free men necessitates contingency (options or choices). If God had fed Adam from the tree of life without telling him of its consequences, Adam's right to contingency would have been taken away from him. Being a free agent and person, eternal life may have been something Adam didn't want. (2) Had Adam eaten of the tree of life ignorantly it would have been a deceptive induction into the Kingdom of God and his contingency lost forever. (3) The tree of life symbolizes Christ. This carries with it the idea of the highest potency of life (Zoe-type life) that solely belongs to God (1 Tim 6:16; Rev 22:2; John 10:10). (4) In Revelation 2:7, Jesus promises that to those who overcome He "will give to eat from the tree of life." Having not yet overcome it, Adam could not have already eaten from it.

How was God accomplish His purpose, then? He could not convert Adam by force, nor by deception, nor could it be automatic; it must necessarily be a gift. Why would God want to give man this great and awesome blessing and privilege?

8.8 GOD'S PURPOSE FOR MANKIND

God wanted to have sons—good sons and daughters. God wanted to give his creatures the ability to partake in the divine fullness of His life. Yet, He did not want to make other "gods" but "sons of God." As Hebrews 2:10 indicates,

For it was fitting for Him, for who are all things and by whom are all things, in bringing many sons to glory, to make the captain of their salvation perfect through sufferings.

The Spirit-Filled Bible says the following about this relationship:

> "There is a profound unity between Jesus and those He saves. We are brethren because in physical birth Jesus shares our descent from Adam, and in the new birth, believers become members of the family of God" (Hayford, 1874).

Romans 8:29 says God determined that Jesus would be "the firstborn among many brethren." This was the highest desire of God, that His infinite expression of excellence and goodness would culminate in the extension of His glory, the perfection of His nature to all. The question was how to achieve this freely?

Adam like all men was given a choice to trustingly obey God. His actions would declare God's right to rule over him as Creator, as Father, and as Sovereign Lord. Adam had to be willing to deny His autonomy instead of God's will. As head of the human race, Adam made that choice for all of humanity. Adam had to demonstrate with his choice that: (1) He believed in God, (2) He loved and trusted God's character; (3) He desired to be a "good son." Adam's faith in God's character is revealed in His Word. Faith is therefore seen as a love response to God. So Adam had to make a choice in which Adam's true goodness could be ratified or confirmed both to himself and God. A love response would "raise man [from] his ethical inclination [or instinct] to the point of choosing for the sake of personal attachment to God alone" (Vos, 42). This is the stuff "good sons" are made of! Dr. Geerhardus Vos affirms this high ideal for humanity.

> *To do good and reject evil from a reasoned insight into their respective natures is a noble thing, but it is a still nobler thing to do so out of regard for the nature of God, and the noblest of all is the ethical strength, which, when required, will act from personal attachment to God without for the moment inquiring into the more abstruse reasons. The pure delight in obedience adds to the ethical value of a choice (Vos, 42-43).*

Does the Lord test us? Deuteronomy 13:1-3 speaks right to the point: If there arises among you a prophet or a dreamer of dreams, and he gives you a sign or wonder, and the sign or the wonder comes to pass, of which he spoke to you, saying, "Let us go after other gods...and let us serve them, you shall not listen to the words of that prophet or dreamer of dreams, for the LORD your God is testing you to know whether you love the LORD your God with all your heart and with all your soul."

8.9 THE BELIEVER'S CONFIRMATION (ESTABLISHED)

In redemption through Christ by the indwelling gift of the Spirit, we receive the "incorruptible seed" which abides in us. To be made pure is to be born again. "For by one offering he has perfected forever those who are being sanctified [set apart]" (Heb.. 10:14). This means that we are made good and are being made good. We are being confirmed in goodness as we follow Christ through the daily choices we believers make in life. According to 2 Corinthians 3:18, the process of being glorified works in us. (For glorification see John 17:5, 22.)

The apostle Paul in 2 Corinthians 3:18 says, "We are being transformed... from glory to glory," from one level of goodness to the next. As we learn to love goodness, conversely, the hatred of evil grows. Sanctification is preparing God's Bride and adorning her with raiments of white, and jewels of rare worth. The following two verses confirm this:

Proverbs 4:18 "But the path of the just is as the shining light, that shineth more and more unto the perfect day." (KJV)

Philippians 1:6 "...being confident of this very thing, that He who has begun a good work in you will complete it until the day of Jesus Christ... And this I pray, that your love may abound still more and more in knowledge and all discernment."

It has been said that God gives us many chances to choose, to Him or from Him. Our obedience ratifies both for God and for ourselves our desire to be "good sons and daughters," that we freely surrender our lives, living in true and eternal benevolent love.

What first appears as a loss of our rights and a loss of freedom, in reality, is the beginning of true freedom. In heaven, we will have given away our right to choose our desires over

God's will. We will have demonstrated by our choices—by the life-long choices of following God's will over choosing to do our own—that we desire to live with God, eternally related to Him as "good sons and daughters."

The change in our nature and our substance is one from abasement to glorification, from mortality to immortality, from corruption to incorruption, which is of such an immense proportion that God wants us to fully understand its implications. For this reason, God gives man 70 to 120 years to realize two things: (1) for the lost to recognize their great need for God, and (2) for the redeemed sons or daughters to confirm their desires to live with God in such a state that they are no longer free to turn away from Him or turn against Him. Then we truly will have become like the angels who can no longer die, for we will have become children of the resurrection. (See Luke 20:36.)

Jesus as the New Head of the human race, as the Second Adam, also had to be tested. Jesus also underwent the confirmation of His "goodness." The human soul that He received was a new, undefiled soul and had to be tested. Unlike Adam who was tested only once and fell, Jesus was tested many times but never fell. In the wilderness, he was tempted by the devil in three areas: (1) as to distrust the providence of God, (2) to presume on the relationship with God, and (3) to achieve God's ends through His ability. Throughout His entire life Jesus was tested and in the process "learned obedience."

Adam's Sin

Adam failed to demonstrate his faith and trust in God, and in God's promise to provide for them a satisfying, meaningful, and fruitful life. The punishment was swift and commensurate with the extended knowledge of God that Adam and Eve possessed. Rather than being confirmed in goodness and being allowed to eat of the "tree of life," they were given over to a sinful (selfish) and unbelieving heart.

Discussion Questions

1. Regeneration is the act and process of restoring to us that which was lost: converting us to the original image of God, in what theologians call the "essential image of God," We are being restored unto knowledge. What does this mean to us as believers? What kind of knowledge is being restored? How was it lost?

2. The character of the new man is also described in Colossians 3:12 as "... the elect of God, holy and beloved, put on tender mercies, kindness, humility, meekness, long-suffering; bearing with one another, and forgiving one another... Above all these things, put on love which is the bond of perfection." This is a description of the "new man" in Christ. How are you progressing with our transformation? Can you imagine Adam and Eve with these temperaments?

3. Adam, though morally pure, was still subject to temptation and therefore vulnerable to sin, and therefore—vulnerable to death. How did God want to move them from this state of vulnerability to complete possession of his blessed condition?

4. Immortality in the philosophical sense expresses the idea of the persistence of the soul, which even when the body is dissolved still retains its identity and its existence. How is Biblical immortality defined in comparison?

5. The most important principle in this course is the concept of being "confirmed in goodness." How is this book's version different from the Calvinist notion of "confirmation"?

Bibliography

Hodge, Charles. *Systematic Theology*. 3 Vols. New York: Scribner & Sons, 1989.

Calvin, John. *Institutes of Christian Religion,* London, England: John Knox Press, 1960.

Hayford, Jack, Ed. *The Spirit-Filled Bible,* Nashville: Thomas Nelson Publishers, 1991.

Vos, Gerard. *Biblical Theology, Old and New Testament.* Grand Rapids: Wm. B. Eerdmans Publishing Co, 1959.

Chapter Nine

THE MYSTERY OF SIN

This chapter deals with one of the most critical and yet most puzzling events in all of history. God, having placed two extraordinary trees in the Garden, told Adam that they would surely die if they ate from one of the trees. God wanted to give Adam and Eve eternal life, an existence in which Adam would no longer be susceptible to sin, and therefore no longer susceptible to death. God's purpose was to make Adam a "son" (*huios S 5207*) of God, an undeserved status and existence far greater than what they had by virtue of creation. Adam was to evidence his desire for God by a simple act of obedience. The evidence would be proffered by an act of faith. This declaration of Adam's will would have confirmed (sealed or ratified) that Adam wanted to be a *huios* of God.

Adam does not make this decision in a vacuum. There are "vested" interests in the decision that he needs to make when Even offers him the fruit of the forbidden tree. Evil is also present in the persona of Satan who was hostile to God's plan of making mere creatures into "sons of God" (Job 4:12-20). The fact that Adam and Eve were given dominion over the earth, coupled with their state of happy innocence caused envy to work in Lucifer's heart until he finally resolved to work for their destruction (JFB Vol 1:50).

Another "mitigating" circumstance is Adam's relationship with Eve. Her beauty and his strong attachment to her were strong motives to listen to her. The situation is a real one, full of all the complexities of human behavior. Involved in the drama are all the major players: God, Adam's new and spectacular bride, and Satan. Adam's equilibrium is off balance by the disturbing suggestion by Eve, which at once both repelled and attracted him. Here is the story of the all too familiar struggle of man's choices, the struggle with himself and with the world.

The story of Adam's fall must be told in three parts. First, we will analyze the cunning and deceptive role the serpent played, and second, how that affected Eve's decision. Third, we will ask some provocative questions about Adam's role in the fall. We will begin by looking at the cunning work of the serpent.

9.1 THE SERPENT

Genesis 3:1 "Now the serpent was more subtle [cunning] than any beast of the field which the Lord God had made."

In a non-religious context, "Cunning, crafty or subtle" has carried the meaning of "clever" (*panourgian S 6175*) meaning one who is capable of anything. Dr. Kittle says this about the word,

The idea that man may have something of *panourgia* about him and yet still be respected might have a special appeal to "sophisticated spirits" since it borders on the power to manipulate others, often without their knowledge, as in deception (Kittle, 722).

In a positive vein, it might mean one who is prudent or full of ability (see Prov.14:24). Its biblical use is predominantly a negative one (Luke 20:23). Spiritually speaking the origin of the world, "cunning" takes us back to the celestial world of the angels. We know that the malevolent spirit in this story had been given incomparable gifts as part of his equipping for the work of the Kingdom. Among those gifts was the gift of wisdom. Ezekiel 28:3-5 says,

Behold! Thou art wiser than Daniel; there is no secret that they hide from you! With thy wisdom and with thine understanding thou hast gotten riches and hast gotten gold and silver into thy treasuries (KJV).

Then the unthinkable happens. Sin entered the heart of this cherub and the wisdom gift was corrupted. Ez. 28:17 says the following,

Thine heart was lifted up because of thy beauty. Thou hast corrupted thy wisdom by reason thy brightness (KJV).

His great beauty was transformed into a red serpent, the symbol of burning sulfur and hate; his great wisdom also converted to its counterpart, "Cunning". Thus the fallen angel falls in love with himself and his beauty. Imagine a being with perfect wisdom, perfect pitch, perfectly adorned with the jewels of virtue. He became the archetype of all narcissists. As Satan, he not only attempts to rob God of His glory but also attempts to rob a man of his glory defacing the image of God in man. This is the fulfillment of perfect envy, that produces not only hatred but murder, and that's exactly what he does. He sets out to murder, rob, kill or destroy. This Satanic principle is at the heart of all disobedience in the Bible, including Israel, who prostituted herself by using the gifts that God had given her for her own wicked desires. Today, fallen man still robs God of his due when he uses the divine gifts and talents of nature and temperament to glorify himself rather than God.

Dr. Dan Fuller says, "The serpent's strategy was a simple one. It was to foster a sinful, unbelieving heart" by confusing and obfuscating the truth (Fuller, 179; Hebrews 3:12). This clever spirit in Luke 20:23-29 is seen when the Pharisees "plot" to catch Jesus by stealth. The Pharisees approach Jesus with the question, "Teacher," they say, "is it lawful for us to pay taxes to Caesar or not?" Jesus perceived their craftiness (*panourgia*) and deals with their treachery. Having failed at their wicked attempt to trap him, the Sadducees approach him, asking,

> *"Teacher...Moses wrote to us that if a man's brother dies, having a wife, and he dies without children, his brother should take his wife and raise up offspring for his brother. Now there were seven brothers, and the first took a wife and died without children. And the second took her as a*

wife and he died childless. Then third..., etc., last of all the woman died also. Therefore in the resurrection, whose wife does she become? For all seven had her as a wife."

In both instances, the questions were designed to impeach Jesus' authority and His influence. In one case it was to embarrass him and in the second it was to give him a question he couldn't answer yet at the same time get him to acknowledge that life continued after death, a hot topic of dispute between themselves. Corporately, they wanted to "divest" Jesus of the glory He was beginning to demonstrate by confounding Him with riddles and insinuations. Jesus charges them with "shutting heaven against men" or "taking away" the keys to the knowledge of the kingdom. We see the evil spirit at work, outwardly appearing righteous while inwardly full of iniquity and death. With true wisdom, Jesus unravels their questions, and they dared not question Him anymore for fear of exposure—exposing the real spirit they represented.

9.2 EVIL CONTEXTUALIZED

Satan approaches Eve, not as an angel of light, but as one of the animals of the field. Satan displays his predatory skills in choosing this disguise, something within the context of Adam and Eve's daily life. An approaching snake would have been a natural occurrence. A talking snake might not have been that unusual to her, after all, she had not been the one that observed and named the animals as Adam had. Conversely, if the serpent had appeared under the guise of an angel of light, it could have potentially convinced her that this messenger was sent by the Lord. So the serpent chose something with whom she would have no trouble accepting.

In this vein, Satan's strategies are often weaved and cloaked in "human ideas and forms" so that the child of God must operate with full discernment as to what they see and hear. Jamison, Fausset, and Brown make the following comments,

> *The whole conversation of the serpent indicates a vile scheme of seduction, designed to make the human pair discontented with the wisdom and goodness of the Divine arrangements as to their condition and to fill them with an ambitious desire to make themselves higher than God...* (JFB, Vol. 1:51).

Satan has only one chance to succeed. If Adam or Eve believe and trust (obey) God they will be confirmed in goodness and granted eternal life. In this case, Satan's goal of separating man from God through sin would have been eternally overturned. God would have executed justice, condemning Satan to the abysmal waters of the Lake of Fire. The stakes are truly high.

9.3 THE DECEPTION OF EVE

After carefully planning his strategy, Satan begins by approaching the "weaker vessel" (1 Peter 3:1; 1 Cor. 11:8-9). Thus the first skirmish in the battle against the human race is between the devil and the woman (Rev 12). Eve's innocent encounter begins with a wrestling match (Eph. 6). Did God say they could not eat of all the trees in the garden? Here we see the push and pull of all demonic temptation.

The serpent begins by quoting God, subtly shifting the words. "Has God indeed said, 'You shall not eat of every tree of the garden?'" The interrogative form expresses surprise. "Really? I can't believe it!" A slight sarcasm serves to refer to some hidden knowledge as if Satan knows something about the garden that she doesn't know, some form of knowledge that God has withheld from her, His beloved daughter.

Instantly she is put on the defensive, feeling foolish and caught off guard. Adding to Eve's confusion, Satan uses the impersonal name for God, "Elohim" rather than Yahweh, the personal name she knows. Surprisingly, when Eve answers, she also uses God's impersonal name, "Elohim," distancing her from the personal use of God's name, which serves as a psychological mechanism to separate her from her Creator.

The structure of the tempter's question confuses Eve. God had said, "Of every tree in the Garden, you may freely eat, but one," the emphasis being on God's gracious character. "I have given you all the trees, except one." Instead of turning away or resisting the serpent as she should have done (Eph. 6:11-16). Eve tries to reason with the Devil even to go so far as to defend God's rules, "We may eat of the fruit of the trees of the garden." Note that Eve leaves out two significant adjectives "every and freely".

Eve then volunteers useful information, "But Elohim did say, 'We may eat the fruit of the trees of the garden, but of the fruit of the tree which is in the midst of the garden, God has said, You shall not eat it, nor shall you touch it, lest you die.'" We see Eve getting slightly confused, first, she locates the tree of the knowledge of good and evil in the center of the Garden though the text does not specifically state this (Gen. 2:9). Eve then adds to God's commandment by saying, "We are not even supposed to touch it, let alone eat of it, lest we die." The added emphasis on Eve's part indicates that she understands the prohibition.

Satan, sensing Eve's untested trust in God, begins the final part of the argument "You shall not surely die." This particular argument might have appealed to Eve's concept of God. Would God really take their lives? Did the crime fit the punishment? "No!" says the serpent. "You will not surely die!" Implied could have been the argument, "God is just, fair and would not use such extreme measures." This is one of the rationalizations men use to divert the possibility of God's wrath against sinners. We judge sin by our own standards rather than God's.

The Devil's objective is something like this: Help Eve to see how attractive the tree and its fruit are, how this coincides with her desire to be more like God, whom she loves, and throw shade on God's willingness to turn them over to death. Jamison, Fausset and Brown say,

It was, however, a direct, infamous lie—a lie told in opposition to his own dire experience; ... that he might have the malignant satisfaction of seeing the human pair involved in the same kind of perdition that he was in (JFB, 51).

In others words, Satan himself was a walking deadman—a living personification of death, of "dying, you shall surely die." Sensing that Eve's curiosity and desire had been adequately stirred up, Satan strikes the final blow by openly declaring that the only reason God has forbidden them to eat of the tree of the knowledge of good and evil God did not want them to share in the abundance of a god-type life. The Devil weaves a web of orchestrated lies using the same core words God had spoken.

8.4 ISSUES OF ULTIMATE REALITY

In asking Eve, "Is it true that God said you cannot eat of every tree of the Garden?" Satan did several things: 1) He suggested that Adam and Eve were not truly free but restrained in some manner by God to their detriment—thereby changing the nature of man, and 2) Satan suggested that God was withholding blessings from them and not sharing with them the river of his delight, thereby changing the nature and character of God. 3) Eve is reminded of the one exception that God has made and mistakenly identifies the tree as being in the center (the implication is that this is the most important tree in the Garden) but as a matter of fact, it is the tree of life which the author of Genesis said was in the midst of the Garden (Gen. 2:9) and as such was to be seen as the most important tree. The use of a comma, which locates the trees, introduces a separation of thought through its construction.

In one fell swoop, Satan's second statement to her has resulted in a new view of the second tree. Instead of being something that would "cause them to die" it was now seen as "something to die for," seeing it as something which would bestow upon them unseen powers and delights—which they had to have—a sort of "expansion" of the life they now experienced in the presence of God. The forbidden tree now represented happiness instead of death. Eve saw fulfillment in it, wisdom and purpose instead of death and separation from God. This is the final and culminating blow—it changed and obscured the nature of sin. (Remember Dr. Fuller's words, "Whatever people believe will make them happy, that they put their hope in.") After this, Eve saw the fruit as good—able to make one wise.

It is good to remember here, that it was not the fruit that was poisonous, but the act of disobedience that caused them to die. This is not a fairy tale of a poison apple given out deceptively by a wicked stepmother which will cause the princess to die. No, this is a choice of disobedience on the part of one of the chief characters in the history of mankind: Adam.

9.5 ADAM'S ROLE

We should ask what was the role of Satan in Adam's fall? We know that God wanted to test Adam, to bring him to confirmation. We have explored in previous chapters why the test was necessary. We should remember that there is a distinction between testing and temptation. Testing, from God's point of view, is an opportunity to self-deliberate, to choose and decide, which is in keeping with man's rational and personal nature. Temptation, however, is looking at the test from Satan's side. Temptation is always with guile, a desire to make one disobey and negate one's values. Satan's purpose in getting Adam and Eve to yield to the temptation is not just to rob mankind of God's blessings, but to bring us more deeply under his control as in Judges 16:5-6, "Show us the secret of your strength, so that we may bind and afflict you." In this regard, one event can be both testing (from God's side) and temptation (from Satan's side).

It appears from the text that Eve listened to a real serpent in a face-to-face conversation, with breath passing through flesh, and not a spirit-to-spirit conversation as the temptation of Jesus may have been. Why do we say this? Because had Satan spoken directly to Eve's spirit, we would not have a clear representation of the source of evil, as coming from the outside, from an external source. That is to say, the source of sin in the primordial couple was not of their design or their natures. Textually this is born out when Eve says to God, "The serpent deceived me." Had the serpent spoken directly to her spirit, she may have said to God, "I had these thoughts, this idea about the fruit, and I ate of it...." A sort of "I deceived myself!" The physical symbol of a serpent is meant to tell us that the primordial couple did not imagine these thoughts, nor were they capable of such thoughts by themselves. The introduction of sin into the human drama is from the "outside" or something external to themselves. For this reason, we say, that though sin is a horrific condition, it is not incurable. It is external to the way God made us. Such being the case, it must therefore be cloaked, delivered by stealth, and must be skillfully contextualized so that the "deceived" or "ensnared" does not expect any serious threat from without. Easily deceived, Eve now easily persuades her husband, Adam, to go along with it.

9.6 THE DECISION OF ADAM

Only common experience can help us understand the emotional tumult that Adam must have experienced when he realized his wife had eaten the fruit of the forbidden tree! Eve's recital of her conversation with the serpent was just the beginning as Adam listened closely.

Remembering that the first couple were real human beings, might the discussion have sounded something like this? Greatly animated, and thoroughly convinced of her position, Eve might have announced "*It wasn't true what God had said* about the tree!" It wouldn't hurt them as they had been told, on the contrary, it was good for food, beautiful to look at, and it would make them wise. Additionally, she might have assured him that the serpent had told her that they wouldn't die! Even though she had eaten, she was still alive! Excitedly she might have continued, "Wouldn't it be wonderful to have the knowledge that God himself possessed?" (Gen. 3:22) Her ultimate strike may have been this argument, "And look, Adam, I'm not dead. I'm still alive." It was true. Eve was standing before Adam, neither physically nor spiritually affected. She was standing naked before Adam and was not ashamed. No doubt Adam's head began to swim—the knocking of sin literally at his door.

As Adam listened to Eve, he may have reeled under the implications of her words. He had never heard such incredible suggestions before! His mind staggered beneath the weight of the options and possibilities! Furthermore, there was hot pressure pulsing through his mind and body as the surging power of wickedness coiled slowly throughout his being. He undoubtedly asked, "Could this be true? Might God be restraining us in some way?"

Jamison, Fausset, and Brown say the following about the nature of temptation:

The history of temptation and every sin is the same, the outward object of attraction, the inward commotion of the mind, the increase and triumph of passionate desire, and the ending is the degradation, misery, and ruin of the soul (JFB, Vol 1:51).

Perhaps, as Adam continued in an unabated silent discourse with himself, he says, "What does it mean that we would become like God? Aren't we already like Him? After all, we are made in His image!" Eve insisted that he eat too and that the proof of her argument was that she had not died. Nothing had yet happened that fulfilled God's dire warning. Perhaps this was the final blow, and this evidence demanded a verdict! "It is true," thought Adam, "nothing has happened to Eve." Furthermore, Eve's beguiling smile and enthusiasm beckoned him on, Adam taking the extended branch from Eve's soft hand, ate, "...Yielding to the arguments and solicitations of his wife, whose insinuating influence prevailed over his better judgment" (JFB, 1:61).

Note, by eating the fruit of the forbidden tree, Adam, quietly elevated the creature over the Creator. 1 Tim. 2:14 says that, unlike Eve who was deceived Adam was persuaded!

In Genesis 3:17 God said to Adam, "Because you have listened [Hebrew, *akouo*] to the voice of your wife and have eaten of the tree that I commanded you not to..." God points out the transgression. In "listening" to his wife's voice, it was not just the hearing of her voice, as in sense perception, but a listening that is reminiscent of Matthew 7 where the wise man who "heard" the words of Jesus, believed them and acted upon them. *Akouo* and the Hebrew associated word group signify a moral and religious dimension—it is "to hear" in the sense of "to obey". The sense of Gen. 3:17 is saying, "Because you obeyed your wife rather than Me." The word *akouo* is also used to describe the obedient relationship between Jesus and the demons (Mk.1:27) as well as over nature (Lk. 17:6). It is also used to describe the believing state of Christians as consisting of a life of obedience(Kittle, 122). The New King James Version of the Bible more correctly translates it as "Because you heeded the voice of your wife...." In Genesis 4, Adam had not simply heard his wife's words and heard her conclusions, but he believed her words over and against the voice of the Lord and then acted accordingly.

Note that Satan's strategy had been perfectly (cunningly) contextualized so that Adam would receive it and believe it. It didn't come through an angel of light but through an angel of flesh and blood—through his wife. What placed Adam in particular vulnerability to the serpent's accusations? Did he have a particular vulnerability when it came to Eve? The answer is yes! It was not Adam's love for Eve that was at stake here, but the Lordship of Jehovah. Was man willing to be ruled by faith in God's tender mercies and benevolent love or by the creature, i.e., by those who can easily influence and persuade us, particularly those closest to us?

Was this not the whole event in God's mind, when God swearing to Himself, discovered that Abraham was willing to sacrifice his only beloved son? Did not Abraham evidence the faith and trust that pleases God? God said to Abraham, "Now I know that you love me," "and on this basis, I will build my people (Gen. 12:1-3). This is also what God wanted to hear from Adam—a "nevertheless your will be done, not mine" as Jesus declared on the night of His greatest temptation in the Garden of Gethsemane.

We must remember that we are like Adam—in a state of probation and the grand design which God has in view in placing us amid circumstances of temptation and trial determines whether we have the faith to obey. From the creation of the world, the grand contest has been, who shall be worshipped and who shall be served the Creator or the creature?

As the two slinked away from the presence of God, the body language of both revealed shame never felt before. Filled with guilt as they walked with their heads down, a heretofore unknown body posture! They were used to walking with their heads held high, regal, and full of glory. Now even their countenance was darkened by the pulsating presence of evil, creating psychological darkness which was near to blindness. The earlier pronouncement of "it is good" left them, leaving them bankrupt of security, joy, and direction.

Hence the strategy of the evil one was subtle and swift, having identified the weakness of Adam's heart. Satan could have used another instrument besides Eve, but he sensed that Adam had a particular vulnerability to Eve. After all, hadn't Adam waited a long time before Eve's appearance, as Abraham had waited for his promised son, Isaac. Satan understood Adam's peculiar vulnerability to Eve. We think that Paul must have seen it in the same light which clarifies his remarks about women.

9.7 THE ROLE OF WOMEN

Paul exhorts women to "submit to their husbands" yet hastens to add an equally stern warning to men, "But love them as Christ loved the church!" No small task here! This is a great mystery, as Paul calls it. He also broadens the scope of his admonition to women in 1 Cor. 11:10-11, "For this reason, the woman ought to have a symbol of authority on her head, because of the angels."

Paul is thinking of fallen angels, one of whom (Satan) took advantage of Eve in the garden. Lastly, the two most controversial of all Paul's words are 1 Cor. 14:34, "Let your women keep silent in the churches for they are not permitted to speak, but they are to be submissive, as the law also says. If there is anything they desire to learn, let them ask their husbands at home. For it is shameful for a woman to speak in church." 1Tim. 2:11-12 says the same, "And I do not permit a woman to teach or to have authority over a man, but to be in silence." Understanding the scene in the garden, we should be able to distill the meaning of these verses in their proper purpose and meaning.

For Paul, the controlling theme is "authority over a man" in the sense of determining apostolic doct<u>rine. Now, "Doctrine" is not seen as a body of knowledge to be handed down from one generation to the next, but as part of the powers of "binding and loosing" that was given to the church by Jesus</u> in the transference of the "keys to the Kingdom." Jesus had taken the keys to the Kingdom away from the Sanhedrin and given them to the apostles. Meaning that the doctrinal authority to declare something valid, good or evil was given to the church from this time onward. Paul's concern during this critical formation of the early church was women were involved in the shouting and the working out of doctrine because there was as yet no "formal agreement" on many doctrinal issues.

What is in focus in Paul's mind during the critical formation of the church is most likely the ease with which Eve convinced her husband of "truth" and with what ease Adam abdicated his responsibility. (It was the same kind of ease that Sarah had in persuading Abraham to take matters into his hand; Samson and Delilah, Rebecca and her son, Jacob, etc.) This is an issue of nature. Women, by nature, are (1) trusting, easily deceived, and (2) encouragers, i.e., born with the power of persuasion in their gifting capacity as "helpmates," while men by nature are susceptible to their charms and their powers of persuasion. This was not a case of arguing substance or value, since it was Paul himself who said that in Christ there were neither male nor female (morally and intellectually) equals before God, but an issue of male susceptibility and female ingenuity. (Hayford, notes on Genesis 3)?

Because of this, many questions quite legitimately arise. What are the implications for women in ministry? On the positive side, we know that Eve (woman) was to be an "*Ever*" to her husband. She was born to be a colleague and a companion in the task of subduing the earth. Eve had a legitimate responsibility in this effort under God. All too many women long to abdicate their responsibility in the proclamation of the Gospel. (This may be good Muslim or Mormon theology, but it is not biblical.) There were equal problems in men abdicating their God-given leadership roles because of sin. They often fail to take spiritual headship in the family. In other words, sin in man robs man of the spiritual fortitude of leadership. Man would, if truth be known, would rather be led than lead. Furthermore, women tend to be creative and quick thinking, she too often wants to take more responsibility than they should. The mix is just too volatile for Paul's liking.

To complicate issues, the Holy Spirit gives to whom He wills all manner of gifts without respect to gender. Hence equipped with motivation and abilities, the godly women must balance Paul's warning with all due reverence and godly fear and seek voluntarily the submission that fulfills Paul's admonition to "cover your head."

What does it mean for a woman to cover her head? It is a wise woman who understands along with Paul, the propensity for abuse and distortion of the delicate balance of power between the sexes. Neither gender appreciates subordination or suppression of their personhood. This delicate balance is worked out however when people live in the Spirit and can easily yield to one another in truth and humility, each person seeking to recognize Christ within the other. In this way, a form of mutual submission occurs in which in-person compliments the strengths of the other. Women must not demand recognition and men must not withhold it. It is the desire to be taken seriously or "listened to" *(respected)* that is sought by women, not a desire to be obeyed (as was the case with Adam who did not only listen to Eve, he obeyed her). With this warning, the Scriptures do not prohibit women to educate, proclaim truth, nor to exhort (prophecy). (See Acts 2:17; 18:26; 1 Cor. 1:5; Phil 4:3; 2 Tim. 1:5; 3:14; Titus 2:3-5).(Hayford Bible, p.1842) So to cover one's head is to cover that part of her that tends to abuse her power: her head. In modern parlance, Paul is saying, "CYA Eve".

9.8 THE TREE OF KNOWLEDGE OF GOOD AND EVIL

Perhaps there is no greater misunderstanding among modern Christians, than the conception of what the "tree of the knowledge of good and evil" represents. For generations, it has been cast in a dubious role. A careful evaluation of the Scriptures will show us something wonderful about this tree. It will reveal a hidden mystery about God's Kingdom.

God said, "Behold, the man has become like one of us, to know good and evil" (Gen. 3:22-23). What does this mean? We know that the tree itself did not possess poisonous fruit. It was not the fruit that turned Adam and Eve into enemies of God, nor did it cause their death. For the tree would rightly have been called "the tree of death" in correspondence with the "tree of life." It is called "The tree of the knowledge of good and evil." Neither is it called the "tree of good and evil." Furthermore, we know that the tree could not have been inherently evil since God is not the author of evil, nor does he tempt man to do evil. So then what is the "tree of the knowledge of good and evil?" Why did God prohibit their partaking of this tree and why does it exist near the tree of life?

Dr. Fuller gives insight into this tree:

It's important to understand what the idiom "knowledge of good and evil" meant. By no means does it mean evil, for God Himself, has such knowledge according to Genesis 3:22, angels have it as in 2 Samuel 11:17 and God gladly gave it to Solomon in answer to his prayer in 1 Kings 3:9. Young children do not have this knowledge (Dt. 1:39; Is.7:15), and the very old have lost it (2 Sam. 29:35). The original readers of the Hebrew understood it to mean a maturity in which they were independent and therefore are fully responsible for the decision they make (Fuller, 182).

Dr. Dumbrell expands and confirms this rendering:

The phrase "knowledge of good and evil" s better taken, following M. Clark, from his book, A Legal Background to the Yahwist's Use of Good and Evil, *as referring to the exercise of absolute moral autonomy, a prerogative which the Bible reserves for God alone. Clark can illustrate the point from a wide range of Scriptures. Solomon for example, prays in 1 Kings 3:9, for an understanding heart to govern His people so that he may discern between good and evil. This is an absolute task before which he is placed, since he continues in the texts, "For who can govern thy great people?" What is clear from this passage is the final authority, decisions of this nature, which affect the whole shape of life, require the mind of God? It must be sought from God and its source must be acknowledged. The regulation of the decision-making processes for life on all levels will not proceed satisfactorily unless the limitations of human knowledge are recognized. By eating the forbidden fruit, the man was intruding into an area reserved for God alone, and the violation of the command was tantamount to an assertion of equality with God, a snatching of deity"(Dumbrell, 99).*

In clear words, "The knowledge of good and evil" was a peculiar Hebrew idiomatic phrase for the _discernment_ between good and evil. When one can discern these, one is wise. Here the tree is a symbol of the wisdom of God, the ability to apprehend reality with divine insight. With the insight that only God possesses—who alone can interpret truth from error. It is equivalent to _Truth which only God possesses._ Before the man could possess such knowledge, he had to possess God—which is represented by the first tree in the Garden, the Tree of Life.

Let us understand this principle from a New Testament perspective: Hebrews 5:11-14 is especially revealing on this crucial point,

> *Of whom we have many things to say, and hard to be uttered, seeing ye are dull of hearing. For when for the time ye ought to be teachers, ye have need that one teach you again the first principles of the oracles of God, and are become such as need milk, and not of strong meat. For every one that uses milk is unskillful in the word of righteousness; For he is a babe. But strong meat belongs to them that are of full age, even those who by reason of use have their senses exercised to discern both good and evil (KJV).*

The author of Hebrews clearly states that strong meat belongs to those who "by reason of use" (they obeyed the word) have their senses (spiritual ears, eyes) exercised (worked, strengthened) to discern between good and evil.

The Old Testament gives us a clue how this works which is embedded in the word *truth, el emet.* There is no one single word for "truth" in the Old Testament, instead, it is said like this, "He who is the truth." Embedded in this word *el emet* is the invitation to verify it by experience—a sort of "Try Me and see if it isn't true what I say." So when one tries it, tests its validity, discovers its truth, and also discovers the knowledge of God in the process. It is a two-fold revelation.

By the obedience of faith, we are given to know the truth, that is, we are fed by the Holy Spirit the delectable fruit of wisdom—the knowledge of good and evil, to know truth from error. In this way, we grow in the knowledge of God. As we eat of the tree of wisdom through obedience, we become like God, knowing good from evil—proving that the fear of the Lord is the beginning of wisdom. Let us look at these verses from the book of Proverbs:

Proverbs 3:13 Blessed are those who find wisdom, those who gain understanding, 14 for she is more profitable than silver and yields better returns than gold. 15 She is more precious than rubies; nothing you desire can compare with her. 16 Long life is in her right hand; in her left hand are riches and honor. 17 Her ways are pleasant, and all her paths are peace. 18 She is a tree of life to those who take hold of her; those who hold her fast will be blessed.

Proverbs 4:5 "Get wisdom, get understanding; do not forget my words or turn away from them. 6 Do not forsake *wisdom, and she will protect you; love her, and she will watch over you. **7** The beginning of wisdom is this: Get wisdom. Though it cost all you have, get understanding. **8** Cherish her, and she will exalt you; embrace her, and she will honor you. **9** She will give you a garland to grace your head and present you with a glorious crown."*

What Adam and Eve had hoped for, the ability to "understand" as God does was completely lost as they plunged into darkness, for the light they had they lost. The lie that Satan told them, "You will become like God" was truly a lie. They did not become like God, they lost their simplicity, innocence, and knowledge of the good. Modern man boasts of having "the knowledge of good and evil" but what happens from the fall is a loss of the knowledge of good. Since the fall we must be told what is good. Unregenerated man boasts of evil and shuns righteousness. Proverbs tells us to seek wisdom, to gain wisdom, for "When wisdom enters your heart, and knowledge is pleasant to your soul, discretion will preserve you and understanding will keep you." God desires us to have wisdom, but not to get it apart from Him. It is important to understand that God's kingdom is synonymous with truth and that this truth or wisdom is personal. It is God through the Holy Spirit. God did not want them to eat of the tree apart from Himself and therefore bans the way back to it.

For Adam to possess such knowledge without God Dr. Fuller explains,

> *Adam and Eve became independent of God by taking matters into their own hands and making their own decisions for their future welfare, the problem here is that man takes upon himself the responsibility of trying (apart from God) to determine whether something is good for himself or not (Fuller, 183).*

Dumbrell follows this line of thinking:

> *The decision of Adam to be self-legislating brought with it diverse consequences. Although thereafter he was the possessor by use of tremendous determinative power, and thus "like God," yet he was "unlike God" in that he would constantly be uncertain of the nature of the issues before which he was placed. He would never be able to foresee the consequences of the choices he would make. Having the power to choose, he would continue throughout his life and history to be the captive of choices. Putting himself in a position of moral defiance to his creator, he plunged himself into a life of tension and absolute moral uncertainty. The command of Gen. 2:17 was not merely probative. In refusing to submit to the moral government of God, he refused to know God (Ro. 1:28). A reprobate mind resulted, and as a consequence of the fall, man became assertive but unable to control himself or his world (Dumbrell, 99).*

It is not an accident that the Bible begins in a garden with two trees and only the tree of life remains. What happened to the other tree? We believe that God planned to give mankind from both trees—life and truth and through their obedience, they would indeed become like God. But Adam had to obey to have this second gift added to him. First, he would have received the "Tree of Life" and then "The Tree of Wisdom". So when he sinned and ate of the second tree, without eternal life, he was doomed to live cut off from God himself—all wisdom lost and in its place independence from God. So for those who have obeyed and are being confirmed in goodness, they can eat of the tree of life now, as they grow wise and enter eternal life with and through Christ. This tree has been fully internalized and lived out. We shall no longer need it for we shall "fully know as we are fully known (1 Cor. 13:12).

9.9 MORAL CONSEQUENCES

> "And when they heard the sound of the Lord God walking in the garden in the cool of the day, Adam and his wife hid from the presence of the Lord God among the trees of the garden."

> "Then the Lord God called 'Adam, where are you?' So he said, ' I heard Your voice and was afraid because I was naked and I hid.'"

Let's look at two evident reactions: Adam and Eve hid from God because they were naked. We understand ourselves, what nakedness means today is a sense of exposure and shame. We quickly cover ourselves when exposed to the scrutiny of the eyes of another. The definition of sin in Hebrew, according to Girdlestone, means to spoil, to break in pieces, and so to be made worthless (Girdlestone, 85). Immediately Adam and Eve sought to cover themselves and endeavored to hide the disgrace of their spiritual nakedness, the natural being a manifestation of the spiritual. Their shame did not have its root in sensuality or any physical corruption, but in the consciousness of guilt before God—an inner shame that their nature had been changed, defiled, and unable to stand before a holy God. They were aware somehow, if only mildly, that the seat of the soul's government now was under the control of a new and evil force. This is the only real shame that man can know—that there is something intrinsically wrong within his being.

God still comes to them as one person to another, searching out the young couple. God gives them the chance to make their confession. The working of sin is already manifest—Adam and Eve immediately offer excuses, each blaming the other. "Adam excuses convince us of a certain coldness, a selfish consideration of his own safety that is of paramount importance" (JFB, Vol 1:55).

Could he shift the blame to Eve, and she perhaps would bear the burden of punishment rather than he? It appears, "He was content to leave his wife to reap the fruit of her misdeeds perhaps making her weakness the perfect scapegoat." The truth in Adam's case was that he had not been deceived. "The reference to his wife's influence was then in no way an excuse, but rather, weak, unmanly and ungenerous," said Jamison, Fausset, and Brown. The image of God in man and his benevolent love for Eve is completely obliterated by his shame and guilt.

Then with daring impiety, Adam tries to throw the blame for his fall, even upon God Himself. His language virtually was this: So long as I continued alone, I was steadfast and immovable in my integrity and allegiance. But thou didst alter my condition; and from the moment I was allied to the wife, whom thou didst provide for me, I found elements of temptation and moral danger in domestic and social intercourse from which I was wholly free in my state of solitude"(JFB, Vol. 1:55).

Was Adam capable of asking for forgiveness? Why didn't they throw themselves at the mercy of God? Their behavior points tragically to the nature of evil and the grip it had upon them. Nowhere do we see Adam repenting or smiting his breast, at least at this point in history, but just the opposite, self-justifying and covering his sin.

This narrative seeks to convey the reality of evil and the grip it has on them and the distortions which result from its hold on men everywhere. "For everyone practicing evil hates the light and does not come to the light, lest his deeds should be exposed" (John 3:20).

Discussion Questions

1. How was Adam's relationship with Eve a mitigating circumstance in his disobedience?

2. Can a gift of God or answered prayer be a snare for the righteous?

3. In the fall of Satan, we see that the gifts of God were not taken from him, but they were perverted and inclined to evil from the moment of his fall. How does this fit with your view of evil and cunning use of knowledge?

4. Satan was successful in Eve's disobedience, what was his strategy in pointing out the one tree that God had forbidden? Does Satan ever point out things to you that causes you to desire it suddenly and without precedent?

5. The tree named the Knowledge of Good and Evil has been given a bad rap in popular Christianity, from a scholarly point of view, what does it mean?

Bibliography

Dumbrell, W.J. *Covenant and Creation, A Theology of the Old Testament Covenants.* Grand Rapids: Baker Book House, 1984

Hayford, Jack, Ed. *The Spirit-Filled Bible.* Nashville: Thomas Nelson Publishers, 1991.

Kittle, *Theological Dictionary of the New Testament,* Grand Rapids: Wm. B. Eerdman's Company, 1976.

Fuller, Dan. *The Unity of the Bible.* Grand Rapids: Zondervan Publishing House, 1994.

Jamieson, Robert, A.R. Fausset and David Brown. *A Commentary Critical, Experimental, and Practical on the Old and New Testaments.* Grand Rapids: Wm. B. Eerdmans Publishing Co.,1973.

Chapter Ten

The Mystery of Grace

The disobedience of Adam and Eve cannot be overlooked or swept under the rug though it may appear that the punishment was unduly harsh. The crime itself was a devaluing of God's authority, His right to rule, and to set the boundaries of good and acceptable behavior before Him. Unlike deists, God did not make the world and leave it to his creatures to decide how to live. Just as in earthly parenting, creation implies a moral obligation to its handiwork.

10.1 THE CURSE (*Arar S 779); (Qualal S7043*)

The first use of the word "curse" is found in Genesis 3:14, 17, "...*cursed* are you more than all the cattle" and "...cursed is the ground because of you." There are various nuances to this word which are all important: First, it refers to a type of "ban" from all other men, and society at large so that there will be no social fellowship between the soul that is cursed and his fellow men or women. Second, it means to bind, he will be stopped from doing the things he wants to do. He will be inundated with obstacles in life, whether occupational, financial, or social. Third, it means that said person will be rendered powerless, his words will carry no weight, made insignificant, small, slight, lessened, weakened, to be lightly esteemed or reviled by others. *Qualal (S 7043)* occurs 130 times in the Old Testament and is the same as the lowering of oneself to a lower state. In other words, the man who sins and is without Christ will never be established. His life and mind will always be double-minded and unstable in all his ways.

Although God does not directly curse man, it is the first time we see man cursing himself through a willful act of rebellion by removing himself from a state of blessedness to a state of involuntary lowliness—thereby crawling on his belly, like his new master, the Devil.

10.2 THE SERPENT'S CURSE

> "I will put enmity between you and the woman and between your seed and her seed" (Gen. 3:15).

God addresses the serpent as the first of the criminals. Even brute creatures are held accountable for their sins. Jamison, Fausset and Brown say,

> *"Being the prime instigator of the rebellion, [he, Lucifer] was to receive no dispensation of mercy, to enjoy no prospect of mitigation... already confirmed in evil, Satan was to enjoy no prospect of restoration, therefore God pronounces on him a sentence of doom, a curse of 'deep and hopeless degradation'" (JFB,55).*

The curse went something like this,

> *Because you have done this, You are cursed more than all cattle, and more than every beast of the field; on your belly you shall go, and you shall eat dust all the days of your life (Gen. 3:14).*

The curse was not to be seen as a curse of evil, but as a prophetic proclamation of God's coming judgment. "Cursed above all the cattle" means that he will be specifically cursed apart from the rest—a prophetic sign of the future life of Satan. Isaiah 14:12 gives us a glimpse of his demise "How you are fallen from heaven, O. Day Star, son of the dawn! How you are cut down to the ground you who laid the nations low! ...You are brought down to Sheol, to the far reaches of the pit." The "sign" must be evaluated within the context of man being the only creature that truly "stands" erect. The animals are made so that either their limbs are bent or their heads naturally point to the ground (a sign of humility). Man is the only one who is erect both in posture and in the natural position of his head. Notice that the serpent does not even have legs, implying that he could not stand if he wanted to, confirming his reprobate status—an irrevocable confirmation of evil.

By implication, those with a serpentine (satanic) character will also be degraded, made to eat from the dust of the ground, unlike their former exalted state, of dining "with the gods" so to speak. It is to be noted on earth, that those who have been morally corrupted are often found among the "unclean" things of the world, lavishing or feasting among the carnal pleasures of the flesh, given over, as it were, to the unclean things of earth, vices instead of virtues—things that pleasure the lower order of man, not the things of his higher nature.

We are to understand that the Lord is not addressing a mere irrational animal, but a knowing being who is morally and rationally aware of his misdeeds. The "going on the belly" is indicative of the lowly position of one who was previously high and lifted up, perfect in all his ways (Ek. 28:16-17) and one who is now "cast down."

All of creation groans from the "fall of man" and not because of a satanic curse but as a direct result of Adam's sin. The curse upon Satan is a separate sovereign act of God. It was Adam, as the "head of all creation" who plunged the world, including the animals, into misery (Ro. 8:20-22). In a sense, it was a curse upon himself. We look to Romans 8:20 in four translations. The keyword to look for is frustration, curse, vanity, failure, and unreality.

> 8:20 For the creation was **subjected to frustration**, not by its own choice, but by the will of the one who subjected it, in hope,... NIV

> 8:20 Against its will, all creation was **subjected to God's curse**. But with eager hope, ... NLT

8:20 For the creature was made **subject to vanity**, not willingly, but by reason of him who hath subjected the same in hope,... KJV

8:20 For the Creation fell into **subjection to failure and unreality** (not of its own choice, but by the will of Him who so subjected it), Weymouth

The earth and all of its inhabitants are subjected to frustration, vanity, and futility. Cain was vanquished to the land of Nod (a type of hell) to live as a wanderer—like a dog always looking for morsels on the ground, endlessly looking for meaning, purpose, materials, life—never at rest. In the end, he would leave everything to another. Eccl... 1:12 says, "Meaningless! Meaningless!" says the Teacher. "Utterly meaningless! Everything is meaningless."

Conversely to be "established" means to have the curse reversed—a life of shalom, nothing missing or broken, a life of well-being and fruitfulness. This reversal may only be found "in the Lord," Look at the following verses:

"And they rose early in the morning, and went forth into the wilderness of *Tekoa:* and as they went forth, Jehoshaphat stood and said, Hear me, O. Judah, and ye inhabitants of Jerusalem: believe in Jehovah your God, **so shall ye be established;** believe his prophets, so shall ye prosper (2 Chronicles 20:19-21).

"For I long to see you, that I may impart unto you some spiritual gift, **to the end ye may be established**..." (Romans 1:10-12).

"Now to Him **that is able to establish you** according to my gospel and the preaching of Jesus Christ, according to the revelation of the mystery which hath been kept in silence through times eternal (Romans 16:24-26).

"Now He **that establisheth us with you in Christ**, and anointed us, is God... (2 Corinthians 1:20-22).

"But the Lord is faithful, **who shall establish you,** and guard you from the evil one" (2 Thessalonians 3:2-4).

The second part of the curse against Satan predicts that there will be irreconcilable enmity (hatred) between the two seeds. This "enmity" refers to the hatred of sin that all believers will have as a result of being in-dwelt by the Holy Spirit. Wanting to maintain order and preserve the life of those who believe, God pronounces an animosity between "her seed" and the "seed of the serpent." We already know that evil hates good because this is the nature of evil. A double principle unfolds, good will also hate evil. This pronouncement essentially sets up the human story of civilization as one of warfare and fierce battle between those who love God and those who oppose Him—the inevitable warfare between light and darkness.

10.3 THE SEED OF THE SERPENT

Just what is the seed of the serpent? Matthew 13:33ff gives us insight into this mystery when it says,

"He who sows the good seed is the Son of Man. The field is the world, the good seeds are the sons of the kingdom, but the tares (weeds) are the sons of the wicked one. The enemy who sowed them is the Devil and the harvest is the end of the age, and the reapers are the angels."

John 8:44 tells us in the words of Jesus, "You are not able to listen to my word, because you are of your father, the devil." The seed of the serpent is seen in the "wicked portion of mankind" which is contrasted with the children or sons of God as in Gal. 3:29 who are "children born not of the flesh but the Spirit" (Also see 1 John 5:19). So we understand that the "seed of the woman" does not only refer to Jesus, who purchased for us the means of salvation, as Gal. 4:4 says, "But the 'seed of the woman' also refers to the Body, to the Church, to all believers in Him, who is in unity with its Head, Jesus. This new head of the human race, 'Who was made of woman' will be glorified, along with His ransomed people (the heirs of salvation) in a better than earthly paradise" (JFB, Vol 157).

Sadly, the two pronouncements that God makes, foresee and predict the human drama that will ensue. The earth becoming the theatre of conflict between the offspring of a woman and the enemy of God (see Rev. 12:9) or a battle between those who adhere to God and righteousness and to those who cling to the Devil in their love and practice of sin.

10.4 THE JUDGEMENT OF EVE—MULTIPLE SORROWS

I will greatly multiply your sorrow and your conception. In pain you shall bring children; Your desire shall be for your husband, and [but] he shall rule over you (Gen. 3:16).

To the woman God prophesies three statements of profound consequence:

1) In pain you shall bring [forth] your children:
2) Your desire shall be for your husband
3) He shall rule over you

To the first point, Jamison, Fausset, and Brown make the following comment:

Other animals, it has been remarked, are commonly in a higher state of health and vigor during the period of gestation than at other times, and bring forth their offspring with comparative ease, while woman forms a solitary exception; the most vigorous of the sex, often being frequently subject to much suffering and even death in the act of giving birth to her children (JFB, 58).

It is not without consideration that the Israelite women in Egypt gave birth easily and frequently, so much so that the

Pharaoh instructed the midwives to kill the boys and save only the girls. The reason he gave was that the Israelite woman (as compared to the women of Egypt) gave birth quickly and without much apparent pain. The nomadic life of pilgrims made the Israelite women stronger than the "excessively domesticated" women (those who were overly indulged in the "good life") of Egypt. God has more than one way to bless his people, the desert hardship proved for their good.

2) Your desire (*teshuwqah S 8669*) shall be for your husband (376 *ishi*)

The root word for desire is *teshuwqah (S 8669)* which means "a stretching out," a "yearning." While these attributes are desirable within their proper context, what is implied here is a "perpetual" yearning, an unsatisfiable longing—a longing that formerly had been filled by God. It also implies that a woman will think that her man can fill these longings within her. Furthermore, it implies that without a man she will suffer from a deep form of melancholia and will acutely feel her aloneness.

3) "And he shall rule over thee..."

To rule *(mashal* 4910) means to "govern, rule, to have dominion." Genesis 1:18 indicates that the sun was to rule over the day and the moon over the night. Men were to have a prominent role in society by ruling. Part of Eve's learning process was to be ruled over by her husband, to learn to submit to his leadership. This is like wearing some of the "hair of the dog that bit you" since she disobeyed her husband. They will reap the fruit of their choices. God will allow what their sinful nature has wrought. Their wild fallen natures will determine how their relationships will unfold.

10.5 THE JUDGEMENT OF ADAM

> "Because you have heeded the voice of your wife, and have eaten from the tree of which I commanded you...cursed is the ground for your sake. In toil, you shall eat of it. All the days of your life both thorns and thistles shall bring forth for you. And you shall eat the herbs of the field. In the sweat of your face, you shall eat bread" (Gen. 3:17-19).

There are several parts to this pronouncement as well.

(1) "Cursed is the ground for your sake..."

As we have mentioned, in Eden the ground had yielded its fruit vigorously. The curse does not fall upon Adam but upon the ground. In a sense, Adam had already cursed himself, but now God's punishment of Adam is seen as a curse upon the ground. The implication of the "thistles and thorns" is that they grow in great profusion in comparison to the herbs and plants. Without great care and cultivation, they would take over the land. Jamieson, Fausset and Brown say,

> "... A single seed of common thistle will produce in the first crop 2,400 and 576,000,000 in the second, and so on

in the same extraordinary ration of increase. Thorns and thistles, which thus possess the natural property of reproducing themselves in so great profusion, are mentioned as prominent parts of the curse pronounced upon the earth for the sin of the first man; and experience shows that weeds of all kinds, particularly thorny on spinous plants... would increase with such or checked by the industry of man" (Fausset, and Brown, 59).

2) "In the sweat of your brow..."

In the "sweat of your brow" shall man eat his bread. This implies the hard work that it will take to overcome the new and hostile properties of the cursed ground. The "sweat of the face" said Jamison, Fausset, and Brown, "...is substituted for the light and pleasant past time" of the Garden experience. The "herb of the field" was substituted for the "delicious fruit trees of Eden" The plants were no longer to be spontaneously produced. The concept of "survival" begins.

10.6 JUSTICE AND MERCY

Why did God choose these particular punishments? The answer reveals God's intimate knowledge of His creatures and simultaneously shows us what He had intended for our particular role in "subduing the earth." Though God does not curse Adam and Eve nevertheless He confirms that it will be impossible for them to find satisfaction in their intended roles.

God's penalty of sorrow in childbirth, sorrow in relationships, and sorrow in doing the work of tending the world reflect the desire of God to prohibit mankind from finding their satisfaction in these things of life, apart from Him. In other words, God knew that woman's satisfaction and contentment were to be found in children and a loving relationship with her husband, but now outside of God's Kingdom, she cannot find it. Likewise man's chief source of pleasure—his work will not give him the desired result, the fulfillment he craves. Although this sounds severe, it is merciful. For if man and woman could find their satisfaction in each other or external interests, the human race would not seek God. We, therefore, need to see that God's pronouncements to Adam and Eve are both penal as well as merciful.

10.7 CREATION GROANS

Several major events occur in the creation of nature as a result of the fall.

(1) Creation and nature—
The damage was done by Adam's decision to disobey God cannot be overstated. For the first time, death and chaos (disorder) entered creation. Remember that the root word of "to sin" (*harmatia*) comes from the concept of "to spoil" or "to disintegrate." Sin, (or disintegration) destroys the sanctity and goodness of the world that God had made. Creation becomes riddled with the disorder. Although creation manifests His glory even after the fall, it also manifests the nature of evil, reveal-

ing something sinister and dark within its lovely branches. The created realm we call "nature" takes on a vicious and sinister reality opposite to its original design: paradise. Is. 14 says that lovely earth became a "wilderness" an inhospitable place. It only takes a brief glance to notice that the world can be a hostile place, i.e., uncontrollable windstorms, hurricanes, floods, tornados, earthquakes, and volcanic eruptions, as well as a multitude of viral and bacterial agents which are lethal and destructive to living organisms, including the man himself. Please notice that we do not use the word "nature" but prefer to use the word "creation," because westerners understand nature as an autonomous reality with its own set of natural laws that operate independently of God. It is far better, and truer to reality, to use the word creation because it inherently implies a Creator. Although man has found a way to protect himself, (from the weather and the marauding bands of animals and men) in the past as well as the present, the earth is still very inhospitable, in stark contrast to paradise.

(2) *Predation*

The whole nature of the animal kingdom has changed as well. The peace that the animal world had enjoyed came to a sudden halt as the ponds that served as mutual drinking grounds became a place for hunting prey. To prove this we can look at Paradise and its total lack of the "chase." The saying, "The little child shall lay down with the cobra and the lion with the lamb" refers metaphorically to the restoration of paradise. The description of the new heaven and the new earth indicates what paradise was like. The restoration of all things includes the animal kingdom. See any wildlife story on television and you will see the stronger overpowering the weaker. In a fallen creation "the survival of the fittest" is a sure thing, not as an evolutionary theory but as the reality of sin.

(3) Zonal Temperature Changes

Not only does the plant and animal life change but according to the general principles of biology, life in a perfect environment of perfect humidity and balance of sun and water would have produced a "terrarium" type environment in which Eden, as well as the earth in general, would have enjoyed a rich and varied vegetative life. The streams of water that had watered the planet provided a steam-like atmosphere that produced tremendously large fauna and flora. This oversized vegetative life could have supported large animals on the scale of dinosaurs. The curse on the ground very likely would have interrupted the interdependent exchange of energy, i.e., oxygen, carbon, etc., causing a rapid change in the atmosphere that would have affected the overall temperature of the earth. It is conceivable that this would have caused drought conditions which would have affected the overall temperatures of the earth. It is also conceivable that this would have caused drought conditions which would have reduced the size and quantity of life. It is likely that after the fall that the flora would no longer support larger animals such as dinosaurs, (whom we believe were originally plant-eaters, and later on became carnivorous). Additionally, water levels likely fell off, perhaps some 100 feet, exposing land masses and draining off available water sources for inland animals. This factor alone could have caused mass extinctions. This could also be an explanation for the freezing temperature which quickly buried land animals and preserved them in their exact form.

(4) Mass Extinctions

According to current scientific findings, there have been many "extensive, and apparently rapid, faunal turnovers (also called mass extinctions) which occurred several times in the history of life (Raup, 14). These extinctions, if true, occurred rapidly, not over long periods as previously thought. Modern science is unable to pinpoint the reason for these drastic changes in nature. From the biblical perspective, we believe that the "cursing of the earth" could have gradually wiped out nearly 50% of all fauna and flora, leaving only relatively few large animals so that by the time of the Noachic flood it is conceivable they could have indeed been taken on a large boat.

(5) Mankind

Man's body underwent a drastic change after the fall. Various commentators have voiced suspicions that Adam originally was quite tall, larger in a muscular frame than today's modern man, which would be consistent with all other forms of created life as being larger than today; growing increasingly smaller since the fall. This theory flies in the face of the evolutionary theory that mankind develops over time into higher life forms.

The Scriptures reveal that all creation groans waiting for the sons of God to be revealed (Romans 8:18-23). Men need redemption but the whole creation as well. When both are restored, God's honor and glory will be fully revealed. God will restore all of His creation, the earth, the heavens, and mankind. That is why the Scriptures promise new bodies, new earth, and a new heaven. Therefore, salvation does not simply refer to the restoration of the human soul, but to restore all of God's handiwork. All of creation must be made anew since it was all affected by Adam's sin.

10.8 GOD'S PROVISION

In responding to their rebellion, by increasing the pain of childbirth for Eve and her daughters, and by making it exceedingly hard for Adam and his sons after him to grow enough food from the thistle-ridden ground, God was showing them the weight of their sin against Him. For God not to have responded to this injustice would be like saying, "You are ok but I am not."

The problem of sin is a legal problem. The punishment must fit the crime. We might ask, who is sufficient to pay the penalty against an infinite God? If the crime involves all humanity, then who could pay this enormous debt? Though everyone is deserving of death, and if all men died, it is not sufficient to pay the debt.

Imagine here the scales of justice. Put God's goodness (glory) on one side and the enormity of evil done. The death of fallen human beings is not sufficient. The sacrifice is blemished and not worthy of God's infinitive worth.

Dr. Fuller continues, "There is no analogy in human jurisprudence where an innocent person bears the punishment a guilty one deserves—so that the guilty one is acquitted and may go free." Yet the Bible speaks of one. Isaiah speaks of one who was:

He was pierced for our transgressions, [who] was crushed for our iniquities; the punishment that brought us peace was upon him, and by his wound, we are healed. We all, like sheep, have gone astray, each of us has turned to his own way, and the Lord has laid on him the iniquity of us all (Is. 53:5).

A sacrifice had to be found which was suitable and acceptable to God. It would have to be a perfect sacrifice, not a tainted specimen of a human being. The sacrifice also had to be a representative of the human race. Jesus, in His sacrifice, fulfilled both of these requirements. The sacrifice had to be administered by a high priest in a heavenly court, not in an earthly realm since the court of justice was the heavenly court of God and the offense was a heavenly offense. It had to take place in the "heavenlies" before all powers and principalities and the whole angelic world. It had to be complete, a once and for all justice. An act which had to take place past, present, and future for in reality we are still sinning against God in our ignorance and are unable to help ourselves.

The justice of an eternal hell must be understood and expressed by the same set of principles. The insult to God's goodness is so great that the death of a sinner is not sufficient to pay for the crime. It is too small a thing to just die once, and it's all over. The crime is infinite, against an infinite God, therefore the punishment is warranted by an infinite amount of "dying," dying the death of eternal death, and fulfilling God's prophecy of "dying, you shall surely die." So we can see four functions as a result of Christ's atonement. He is fully all four—(1) a perfect sacrifice, (2) propitiation, (3) reconciliation, and (4) and redemption. In the first case, man stands as a guilty person before God and a sacrifice is needed or blood needs to be shed. As to propitiation, sinful man is the direct object of God's wrath and exposed to God's anger, and therefore a covering is needed for mankind—Jesus the mercy seat of God. Third, as to reconciliation, sinful man has become an enemy of God and therefore reconciliation between God and mankind is needed. As to redemption, mankind through sin has become the slave of sin and needed a ransom to be paid to set him free from this bondage. Christ has freed us from the bondage of Satan.

Discussion Questions

1. How does the Biblical use of "curse" play out in today's society? How is that tied in with the idea of not being able to be 'established?" What does "established' have anything to do with the idea of "rest?"

2. Have you ever considered the idea of "enmity" as a significant factor in your relationships?

3. The seed of the serpent has one key identifier. What is it?

4. How is Eve's (women) perpetual longing for her husband a just consequence of her sin?

5. There are four reasons included in the sacrifice of Jesus on the cross. Please name them.

Bibliography

Fuller, Dan. *The Unity of the Bible*. Grand Rapids: Zondervan Publishing House, 1994.

Jamison, Robert, A.R. Fausset and David Brown. *A Commentary Critical, Experimental, and Practical on the Old and New Testaments.* Grand Rapids: Wm. B. Eerdmans Publishing, 1973.

Chapter Eleven

THE MYSTERY OF GIFTS

Now we turn to the sons of Adam. It seems that there is an important lesson in this story otherwise the author could have ended this sad saga with the expulsion of Adam and Eve. There is something doctrinally important in this story that begs further exploration.

> Genesis 4:1 "Now Adam knew his wife Eve, and she conceived and bore Cain, and said, 'I have acquired a man from the Lord.'"

At his birth, Eve cried out, "I have acquired a man from the Lord according to His promise." The promise of Gen. 3:15 was very real for Eve for she and Adam were looking for the kinsman-redeemer. It may have been an assumption on Eve's part that Cain would be the representative deliverer. If so, perhaps Cain believed that as well. This could have accounted for his sense of entitlement and subsequent offense at the rejection of his gift. It may have also been something completely natural and fleshly such as being the eldest son and in the direct line of inheritance.

> Genesis 4:1 "Then she bore again, this time his brother Abel. Now Abel was a keeper of sheep, but Cain was a tiller of the ground."

By contrast, Abel means "breath or vanity" in keeping with his short little life. Again like all good narratives, the context of the story is developed through an introduction of their respective occupations, setting the stage for the upcoming drama.

11:1 AN OFFERING

> "And in the process of time, it came to pass that Cain brought an offering of the fruit of the ground to the Lord. Abel also brought of firstborn of his flock and their fat. And the Lord respected Abel and his offering, but he did not respect Cain and his offering. And Cain was very angry and his countenance fell" (Genesis 4:3-4).

Why is Cain's offering rejected? Was it a matter of ignorance on Cain's part? Let us briefly explore this possibility. Now that the ground was to be tilled manually, it was Adam's responsibility to teach his children how to survive in a radically different environment. Part of their training included spiritual matters as well. The fact that Cain brought a gift from the earth makes many ask, was this the reason that God rejected the gift? Did Cain fail to bring an animal offering? Perhaps a lamb had to be sacrificed as a precursor of the Spotless Lamb that takes away the sins of the world and not the produce of the field. Many people teach that God instructed Adam and Eve on the rituals of blood sacrifice to approach God, but the text leads us to believe that the content of their spiritual teaching so far was by grace alone, that is: that God would send help via the promise of a future kinsman (a seed) to deliver them from sin (to crush the head of) their oppressor.

Thus we can conclude that this early sacrifice of Cain and Abel was simply a means of communicating with God as an act of humility, deference, and thanksgiving, each child was trained in the "ways of the Lord" by Adam himself.

What is viewed here is the extravagance of Abel in the quality of the gift, i.e., the "first born of his flock and their fat." It would have been an entirely different picture had Cain brought forth the "first fruits of the ground" and of their ripe, mouthwatering produce which represented the works of his hands, i.e., his life's work. Thus the text seems to say that it was not the gift per se that is judged but the quality of what the gift represents.

Returning to the text, it says that Cain brought an offering of the fruit of the ground to the Lord. This is contrasted with Abel's gift "the firstborn of the flock and its fat." Cain's gift appears to be haphazardly offered while Abel's gift was extravagant (not too extravagant, for what can we give God that he does not already possess)? He took time and made effort in selecting his gift to God. We know from Hebrews 4:11 that Abel *"offered to God a more excellent sacrifice than Cain."* We can surmise that Cain's attitude toward God reflected a certain distant coldness reflected in his off-hand gift. Why did Abel give such a great and acceptable gift to God?

11:2 THE GIFT THAT JUSTIFIES

Hebrews 11 tells us what might have motivated Abel to give the "firstborn and of the fat." Hebrews 11 is about the theme of faith. All of the biblical heroes in this chapter believed that God could be trusted to fulfill His promises. Abel offered by faith. Faith in what? That God was going to fulfill His promise (See Haggai 2:5). They all had a faith in the coming Messiah that made him acceptable (justified) to God. Therefore his joy was full and in that joy, he gave the very best gift he could, one that would have been worthy of a God who would set them free and back in communion with Himself. As we look to the rest of the heroes of the faith we see the same evident theme of trusting God to fulfill that which He had spoken. This is justifying faith. Let's look at this in-depth:

a) Enoch sought God because he believed in the promise that those who seek him, will surely find Him.

b) Noah moved in the faith of the things not yet seen, the promise of salvation through his obedience to build an ark. In a time when there had been no rain, he began his work of faith.

c) Abraham obeyed when he was called to the place he did not know but believed the promise of God to give him a land, a name, and posterity.

d) Sarah believed God (judged him faithful) to give her a child in her old age, even though the outrageousness of the prophecy caused her to laugh.

Abel believed the promise communicated by his parents regarding the coming deliverer. His faith in the promise of a deliverer would account for his delight and gift which obtained him the witness of his righteousness. (Hebrews 11:1)

Faith means trusting in the goodness and faithfulness of God. Abel offers his sacrifice in this attitude. As Dr. Fuller states, "Trust is the greatest gift you can give to another person." It says that this person is true, trustworthy, and merits our faith. It says, "I have judged thee O. God and found you faithful and true." Hebrews 11 is all about faith. Cain's gift did not display this attitude. On the contrary, he judged God to be unfair, displaying the same mental attitude of most unbelievers: rejecting all light except for the light of their reason. He typifies the "natural man" in his approach to God and his self-righteousness.

11.4 THE SALVATION OF GOD

> "...Cain was very angry and his countenance fell. So the Lord said to Cain 'Why are you angry? ...Why has your countenance fallen? If you do well, will you not be accepted?'"

Cain's response was anger. Instead of seeing this as an appropriate rebuke for his lazy gift-giving, he was indignant. Not being accepted was a huge humiliation, being outdone by his younger brother. He had fulfilled the obligation, was anything more needed? Closer to the truth, was he angry at hearing the truth?

"If you do well, will you not be accepted?" Hoping to bring Cain to confession, He reminds the young man gently of His righteous character. God is pointing out that He is just to forgive sins. To be accepted means being justified. Cain could have admitted "Yes, it's true. If I do well, I will be accepted, for you are fair and just. This is how You are—generous, kind, and quick to forgive." For God, this would have been true repentance, and Cain would have been confirmed in goodness, like Abel. He would have been justified, saved, and acceptable to God. Even here we see the redemptive process at work: true repentance is agreeing with God about the situation, giving admission of truth and the need for true transformation.

God knows that Cain's anger has increased to the level of hatred and building toward murder. Yet God tries to restrain him, by speaking the truth and encouraging faith in God's character. But Cain casts aside all restraint, rejecting God's voice. "And if you do not do well, *sin lies at the door*, and its desire is for you, but you should rule over it (Genesis 4:6-7).

Cain is infected with sin, yet he is warned that something external to himself wants to overtake him. By hearkening to the voice of God, he can overcome. It's important to see the remedy that God offers Cain—belief! Obey! Put sin away from you!

11.5 THE POWER OF SIN

"Now Cain talked with Abel his brother, and it came to pass that they were in the field, that Cain rose up against Abel his brother and killed him" (Genesis 4:8-9).

Notice the repeated use of the word "brother". This clearly shows us that not even "family" is a sufficient shield from the power of sin. Second, 1 John 3:12 tells us that Cain was "the *first one who let sin reign in him.*" "He was of that wicked one." Jesus said, "He (Satan) was a murderer from the beginning" (John 8:44). Is this the scene he refers to? We see Satan bring death to Adam and Eve, but in only one generation the full flower of sin has sprung forth in the physical murder of Abel.

"And He says, 'Where is your brother?' He said, 'I do not know. Am I my brother's keeper?'"

The chilling indifference on the part of Cain shows us the beginning of sin. So? Cain says. You can just imagine the feelings that God must have had as he recognizes the spirit in Cain. Yet God shows mercy with his judgment.

"What have you done? The voice of your brother's blood calls out to me from the ground. So now you are cursed from the earth which has opened its mouth to receive your brother's blood from the ground. When you till the ground, it shall no longer yield its strength to you. A fugitive and a vagabond you shall be on the earth. Cain replied to the Lord, My burden is more than I can bear. You have banished me from the land, and from your Presence, you have made me a homeless wanderer. Anyone who finds me will kill me." (Genesis 4:10)

Cain is not sorry, nor penitent, rather he is afraid of being punished, afraid for his own skin, and afraid Adam's descendants will kill him. Cain's response is a selfish concern for himself, how will he live?

"And the Lord said to him, 'Therefore whoever kills Cain vengeance shall be taken on him sevenfold. And the Lord set a mark on Cain, lest anyone should find him and kill him'" (Genesis 4:15).

God's response to Cain's self-concern is twofold. First, it is prescriptive God intends that man should not be the one to take revenge, but that God himself will do the repaying. "Vengeance is mine," saith the Lord. Second, God displays mercy once again. Perhaps the descendants of Cain will recognize their need for God. The mark on Cain then, was not a physical sign on him, but rather, a sign or pledge given to him, indicating the promise God made to him. Here is a promise that Cain is willing to believe!11.6 The Land of Nod

"Then Cain went out from the presence of the Lord and dwelt in the land of Nod, on the east of Eden" (Genesis 4:16).

Nod is east of Eden and means "banishment." Living in Nod typifies the "restless wanderer" a state of being that will befall man all his life, a life without God. Conversely, Eden is the symbol of being in God's presence and for being established as in 1 Peter 5:10, "After you have suffered for a little while, the God of all grace, who called you to His eternal glory in Christ, will Himself perfect, confirm, strengthen and establish you." Cain's descendants lived without thinking of God. They built towns, and invented tools and musical instruments all constructed to help them live a life of pleasure that would dull the pain of separation from God, helping them to alleviate their fears of being alone, fragile, and lost.

11:7 THE ACCEPTABLE WORKS

If Cain's offering was rejected then how are we to judge our offerings before the Lord. What is the rule for kingdom life? The New Bible Dictionary states that the works of man must meet the following standards:

a) The love of God must be the source of inspiration.

b) The law of God set the rules for engagement.

c) The glory of God must be the goal of the work.

d) The motivating power must be the Holy Spirit.

Hence, a good man can do good works, but they are not necessarily in line with God's standard. In one form or another a work becomes a selfish work, a work of the flesh, brought about by evil desires and a law unto itself, rather than a work subjected to the will of God. The *New Bible Dictionary* says,

> "Unregenerate man can do good things, but the motivation for them is not from the love of God. Therefore these works (although in accordance with the law) are not good and well-pleasing to God. They are done from enmity (the carnal mind is enmity toward God) not in accordance with the love of God. Although depraved men can do things according to the law, they themselves are not subject to the law of God" (Douglas, 1960). (See Acts 9:36; Ephesians 2:10; 2 Timothy 3:17; Titus 2:14.)

In review, we see that sin introduced into the world—jealousy, depression, anger, hatred, murder, fratricide, selfishness, indifference, defilement of the earth, punishment, expulsion, the loss of God's presence, and friendship. To those add the terror of the unknown, polygamy, pleasure, and materialism.

Paul in his indictment said, "The carnal mind is enmity against God." (Romans 8:7) The New Bible Dictionary says,

The common notion that sin is selfishness betrays a false assessment of its nature and gravity. From the outset and throughout its development, sin is directed against God and this analysis alone accounts for the diversity of its forms and activities. (Douglas, 1960)

Depravity is sin and always proceeds from a depraved heart. Sin is a perversity of the human heart, mind, disposition, and will. Sin, therefore, has passed on from Adam, and carries with it the perversity of heart. "That which is born of the flesh is flesh" (John 3:6). "The carnal mind is enmity against God" (Romans 8:7).

Discussion Questions

1. After studying gift-giving we know that gifts should be given as indicators of the relationship's degree of intimacy and value. How does Cain's gift reflect his opinion of the Lord?

2. Even though Cain murdered his brother, God tells him three things that indicate God is a God of second chances. What were those three things?

3. Abel's gift which is acceptable to God says what about Abel?

4. What is the land of Nod? In this land, why are men's faces always looking down?

5 Describe what a free act is? What makes them free?

Bibliography

Robert Douglas. *The New Bible Dictionary*, Grand Rapids: Wm.B. Eerdmans, 1962.

Fuller, Daniel. *Unity of the Bible*. Grand Rapids: Zondervan Publishing House, 1994.

Jamieson, Robert, A.R. Fausset and David Brown. *A Commentary Critical, Experimental, and Practical on the Old and New Testaments.* Grand Rapids: Wm. B. Eerdmans 1995, 1973.

Lesson Twelve

The Mystery of Civilization

In the last lesson, we saw the separation of Cain from his parents, his family, and his way of life. We saw how Cain complained about his harsh punishment which God addressed by placing a mark on him. Many believe that the mark was a physical sign placed upon the body or head. Others believe that it was a mental defect or a melancholic spirit.

None of these seem like ideas warranted by the text. It is more likely, that God gave Cain a pledge, a promise, indeed "a sign" that God would protect his life against recrimination rather than consigning him to be a hunted man. This is the principle of the "wheat and the tares" dwelling together until the end of time at which time God alone will separate the sheep from the goats.

As such, we see God's mercy upon Cain (in giving a pledge) as a means of drawing men back to Himself—thereby confirming His readiness to forgive and restore. This sign or "promise" should have been received with a grateful heart, but instead, the promise is distorted by his descendants who have turned it into a matter of boasting. *Lamech* in Genesis 4:24 says, "If Cain shall be avenged sevenfold, then Lamech, seventy-sevenfold."

In other words, if Cain is avenged seven times, how much more will his descendants be protected. Nowhere do we hear that God has made such an extravagant promise to "overlook" or "forgive" sin. The nature of evil, however, is to expand a promise until it allows the sinner to justify his actions of non-compliance with the will of God.

The "titanic arrogance" of sin is seen in the seventh generation, so not even a hint of the fear of God remains. The children of wrath freely flaunt their sin before men and God, without any fear of punishment or retribution. This account is typical of the nature of sin, the perspective of the wicked who believe that they are beyond God's judgment and it is prophesied that it will be like this at the end of the age.

12.1 TWO LINES OF HUMANITY

God sets the course of Cain's destiny by setting his course as a "wanderer," a man without family, without roots. Cain sojourns in the land of Nod, a land that is filled with large beasts and creatures of the wilderness.

Cain defies God's punishment by building a city and naming it after his first son "Enoch." The name Enoch means *"one who initiates."* The building of the city is a way of compensating for the curse of being out of fellowship with God. The city, despite all its achievements, produces a profound sense of loneliness and isolation that men seek to overcome through an abundance of glittering lights and sounds. These "moving" objects, lifeless objects that appear "to live" are a poor consolation for the true source of life.

The line of Cain fared very well in the beginning. There appear to be many significant blessings. In verse 4:17 we read that Cain was immediately blessed with a child, Enoch who proceeded to build a city and name it after his son.

Urban living was a new stage in the development of the human race. Though the dwellers built small gardens for food, gradually there developed different habits, called "city habits." Life in the city enabled the cross-fertilization of ideas, and the development of inventions, and served as a strong impulse for the creative arts. The city founder, Cain, set the tone for the development of future generations, for it increasingly became a population of godlessness, excessive luxuries, and sensual and commercial appetites. The ruin of any modern city is experienced when greed in commerce and corruption of the arts takes hold, impoverishing a community rather than enriching it. God will not be mocked.

At first glance, it would appear that the murder of Abel produced little if any negative consequences. Abel's blood, it seems, was not avenged by God. Conversely, it appeared that his line prospered and that the blessings that accompany righteousness were not a significant loss to Cain and his family other than the immediate presence of God. Over time, that would be easy to eradicate, with all the sights and sounds the city had to offer.

However, a closer look reveals that the "blessing" of Cain's posterity appears to be only a physical blessing or material blessing. A true evaluation of their "success" is apparent when we compare and contrast the meaning of the names his posterity held. A brief reading of the verse will identify the six generations and give us further insight into the nature of their development.

12.2 WHAT'S IN A NAME?

> "And Cain knew his wife and she conceived and bore Enoch. And he built a city and called the name of the city after the name of his son—Enoch. To Enoch was built Irad, and Irad begot Mehujael, and Mehjael begot Methushael and Methushael begot Lamech. And Lamech took for himself two wives: the name of the one was Adah, and the name of the second was Zillah. And Adah bore Jabal. He was the father of those who dwells in tents and have livestock. His brother's name was Jubal. He was the father of all those who play the harp and flute. And as for Zillah, she also bore Tubal Cain, an instructor of every craftsman in bronze and iron. And the sister of Tubal Cain was Naaman" (Genesis 4:17-25).

Adam's choice of a name for his new son, Seth, recognizes a new state of repentance and justification for both Adam and

Eve. Seth means "the appointed one or the compensation for Abel's death." Seth names his son, "Enosh" which means weak, frail, and mortal as compared with Enoch of Cain's line, born in the same generation, "One who initiates or takes control." The names on the Sethian side reveal an increasing awareness of their dependence on God while the Cainian side reveals an increasing arrogance and independence from God.

With the naming of Enosh, the statement "Then men began to call on the name of the Lord" reveals a newly found recognition of their dependence on God and a declared statement of their position toward God, one of humility and gratitude." To call upon the name of the Lord" literally means to worship Him, to trust in Him, and to believe on Him as the sovereign Lord and Creator of the universe. This also means that they began to call upon Him as a "mediator," one who would redeem them from the curse of sin. This is born out of the rest of Seth's descendants' names. We will compare the two lines as indicative of the spiritual state of both lines. The idea of "two lines" is critical in understanding the development of history. History builds from the theological point of view by the choices they make, trust in God, or trust in oneself.

Irad in the line of Cain means "townsman" compared to Jared which means "descended one." The virtue and blessing of belonging to a family and knowing your ancestors go without explanation. There is a greater sense of security and identity *as compared* to a "townsman" who lives in a conglomerate of unrelated people. In this case, we would expect commitment, loyalty, and security to be low as compared to a "family" which gives all to protect each other.

Compare Mehujael in the line of Cain with Mahalalel in the line of Seth. Mehujael means "smitten of God" while Mahalalel means "praised of God." Mehujael experiences the loneliness that comes from being "smitten by God." This involves a total sense of rejection and alienation from the wellspring of life. Psychologically, alienation breeds mental illness not to mention a despondent and melancholic spirit when compared to Mahalalel who enjoys the significance of being "praised of God." Praised of God means "one who praises God" so that others are encouraged to worship and follow Him. His name then means "one with a ministry" giving purpose to his life.

Methushael means "man of the sword" compared with Methuselah meaning "man of prayer." The first speaks of the ways of men, the strength of the flesh, with all of its passions, brute force, and prideful ways, while the other reveals a man who lives a life of peace, seeking and trusting God.

Lamech means "a strong young man" or "a man of titanic arrogance" compared with Enoch who is taken away and does not see death. What is compared here is not so much their names but their outcome. Both are the seventh generation of Adam and represent the outcome of either their ungodliness or their piety and righteousness. Enoch, the culmination of the godly line is so filled with God's spirit that he is literally "taken away" in the seventh generation and never sees death. What is the significance of this for the believer today?

In Jude 1:10-12 we see men who have gone the "way of Cain." The way of Cain is displayed in men/women who have no fear of God and scorn the love and grace of God. The final culmination of this ungodly arrogance (at the end of the age) is best represented by the antichrist who will come against the final culmination of the godly line is Jesus and His seed—the perfected man or woman of God in Christ. We are counted as one with Christ and are marked as their enemy along with its founder, Jesus.

The sons of Lamech, Jabal, and Tubal, say Kiel and Delitzsch, give the impression of one flowing river which signifies the sense of ease and complacency that might more accurately be called the "pride of life." Cain reflects self-concern and self-interest while Enoch of the godly line reflects his concern for the sons of God. His son, Noah, means "comforter of the people." This comfort will only come about after the flood justice has been adjudicated.

12.3 THE BLESSING

What then is the blessing of the righteous? What is it about the blessing that is scorned by unbelievers who continually sneer at the "blessing of Abraham"—the blessing that Esau gave up for an immediate serving of food? What is it righteous cling to, yet does not appear recognizable as the "pearl of great price?"

The blessing consists in a relationship with God that is unseen and eternal, compared with the blessings of Cain which are seen and temporal. God's blessing appears to be simple, easy, and not a blessing because it is not primarily "materialistic" though God does promise land and name (significance). True blessings come from God, that is family, long life, secure life, happiness in the heart and mind, freedom from worry, good sleep, and abundant crops. It is a passive receiving as in the tree which is planted by the side of the brook, finding its nurture in the deep underground waterways (Ps 1).

The blessing in this lesson is seen when comparing the "long lives and many children" as recorded in the lives of those first patriarchs. The sons of Seth lived long lives with many children. While the sons of Cain lived undistinguished lives with no reference to children.

When is the blessing finally visible to the world? It is visible over time. The fruit of righteousness comes in "due season," which is why Paul said, "Don't grow weary of doing good, in due time you will reap a harvest." Conversely, the stain of sin becomes obvious in the lives of people also in "due time" and is visible to the naked eye. In each generation, there is a time of disillusionment as the dreams and promises given by the deceiver are seen for what they are: lies and emptiness, while the believer has not only several blessings but blessings in abundance.

12.4 A REVERSAL OF FORTUNES

In keeping with the two lines of mankind, the Bible continues:

Now it came to pass when men began to multiply on the face of the earth, and daughters were born to them, that the sons of God saw the daughters of men, that they were beautiful, and they took wives for themselves of all whom they chose. Gen. 6:1-2 NKJ

The "sons of God" refers to the line of Seth. There is a remarkable difference between those who "called upon the name of the Lord" and those "who went their own way." There is no reason to think that the author intended to introduce a new theme, as many people have tried to introduce, such as angels coming to earth and interfering in the lives of the human race. Rather, the "sons of God" refers to the line of Seth, "those who called upon the name of the Lord." These very same ones who "saw the daughters of men" that they were beautiful. The sons of God, or the Sethites, took for themselves wives from the line of Cain, i.e., "...The daughters of men." In other words, there was intermarriage.

The objections to the sons of God as referring to angels are many. For one, angels do not marry nor procreate, they are non-material. To introduce inter-breeding between angels and men would change the composition of man and make him into a demigod, rather than a man. This would also change the outcome of history as it no longer consists of a purely human race in need of the Savior's incarnation.

In addition, the text calls for a continued revelation built from Chapters 4-5 in the distinctions or "separation" between the two lines which culminate with the antichrist and Jesus Christ.

> *"There were giants (Nephilim) on the earth in those days, and also afterward, when the sons of God came into the daughters of men and they bore children to them. Those were the mighty men who were of old, men of renown" (Genesis 6:4 NKJV).*

According to Jamieson, Fausset, and Brown, the reference may mean the founders of cities who later became objects of idolatry and subsequently "deified." For instance, *Jubal* was *Jubaal* of the Phoenicians, *Jabal,* and *Jubal* were the Pan and Apollo of the Greeks and Romans; *Tubal-Cain or Tu-baal-cain* became Vulcan from *Vul-Cain*. *Naamah* or in Greek, *Nemano*, became Athena otherwise known as *Minerva*.

The reference to the *Nephilim* (giants) is commonly traced to *naapal*, "to fall" and considered to signify either "fallen ones," "apostates" or "falling upon others." In the first sense, many may attempt to apply it to designate fallen angels. In keeping with the "two-line" theory it is evident that it describes a particular class of men who were marauding nomads—men of a violent, overbearing lawless character—"who abused their bodily powers to obtain their selfish ends; who were constantly roving from place to place in quest of plunder, and emerging suddenly from their retreat made attacks on the property and lives of men" (JFB, I:89,90).

Regarding marriages, they say this,

> *Whether the Sethite husbands, having broken through the restraints of religions, settled in infidelity or were slaves to female influences, they abandoned all care of their households to their worldly and godless partners, a progeny was reared under them, utter strangers to everything sacred and good, without either precept or example to control the outbursts of juvenile passions. Each succeeding race became worse! But the mixed marriages that became so frequent produced a vast increase of violent and lawless characters like the Nephilim, persons of reckless ferocity and audacious impiety, who spread devastation and carnage far and wide (JFB, I:90).*

12:5 GOD REPENTS

"Then the LORD saw that the wickedness of man was great in the earth and that every intent of the thoughts of his heart was only evil continually. My spirit shall not rule in men forever, in their wandering [they have proven] they are but flesh" (Gen. 6:3-5 NKJV).

"My Spirit shall not always dwell or remain in man," forewarning them that the Shekinah or Divine Presence (or the convicting power of sin) would not always be in the world, understanding that unregenerated men are "incapable of being ruled by the Divine Spirit of God." This is the same principle of "shaking the dust from your feet." If your message of good news is rejected, move on, in doing so remove the means of salvation from their midst.

The *Biblical Theological Dictionary* says, "Evil" is broader than just "sin." The root word of sin comes from the word "to spoil" or to "break apart in pieces." (Douglas, 400) When Genesis 6:3 is tied with 6:5 it shows that the "breaking apart of a man" is a spirit that keeps them wandering, much like an animal, coming and going, not knowing whence or where to go like a dumb animal which is the general meaning of the designation of "wanderer" on Cain. God repents (or is sorry) because this is not the purpose for which His creation was intended. He grieved in His heart saying, "I will destroy man, whom I have created from the face of the earth, both man and beast, creeping thing and birds of the air, for I am sorry that I have made them" (Genesis 6:7, NKJV).

That this included the "sons of Seth" is evident in that they "had come under the dominion of carnality and addicted to every kind of wickedness" (JFB, 1993:91).

The line of Seth did what every generation does when it departs from Christ. Disappointed in their hope of the promised deliverer, they grew weary of doing good and abandoned their faith, aided by the "glitter and gay" ways of the Cainites. Gradually then, the whole world filled with wickedness.

Sin became so conspicuous to God (even from their youth) that he could not refrain from judgment. He had intended to fill the earth with his glory by having people made in His image "fill" the earth and having them rule over the fishes, birds, and animals. As a result of intermarriage, the Cainites now outnumber the Sethites.

12.6 THE FLOOD-GOD'S JUDGEMENT

In the 500th year of Noah's life, God told him to prepare an ark. God's patience had come to an end. He worked to execute justice unto all ungodly men (1 Peter 3:20). Into this sweeping judgment would fall the "nations" (tribes) and the natural order. The inhabited earth would come to a complete close—all flesh would die. The previously described landscapes of incredible beauty and creativity would all come to an end. The habitats of all rare and exotic creatures, as well as man, would be destroyed. Bunyan says, "In this, therefore, we have a semblance of the last judgment, and how God will dispose of his friends and enemies (1 Peter 3:20). To Noah he said, "Come thou and all thy house into the ark; for thee have I seen righteous before me in this generation (Genesis 6:7).

By saying these words, God has established the true basis of salvation, saying through Isaiah, "Come, my people, enter thou into thy chambers, and shut thy doors about thee: hide thyself as it were for a little moment until the indignation be passed over (Isaiah 26:20 KJV). "And he shall send forth his angels with a great sound of a trumpet, and they shall gather together his elect from the four winds, from one end of heaven to another." (Matthew 24:31, KJV)

"Come thou and all thy house" meaning, not even a "hoof" must be left behind is reminiscent of John 6:39 says, "And this is the will of Him who sent me that of all that He has given me I lose nothing but will raise it up at the last day." God was careful not only of Noah but of all that were in his house because they were all of his visible church. "Gather my saints together unto me, (saith he) those that have made a covenant with me by sacrifice (Ps. 50:5).

"Of every clean beast, thou shalt take to thee by sevens, the male and his female: and of beasts that are not clean by two, the male and his female. Of fowls also of the air by sevens, the male and his female; to keep seed alive upon the face of the earth" (Genesis 7:1-3).

Thus by the commandment of God, both Noah and all that were with him (clean and unclean) would be saved. His reason for saving the "unclean" remains as part of his covenant with Cain, and the promise to let the wheat and tares grow together. For even amid the boat is the presence of a corrupt soul—Ham—but with the promise made to Cain. "If you do well, will you not be accepted?" This overrides, for us, the belief in predestination to eternal damnation. God, even amid the flood, gives the wicked another chance to turn to Him. Thus we also say "clean and unclean" may be in the church, "Yet one of you is a devil" yet not irrevocably so.

God then speaks to his servant Noah in Verse 4, "For yet seven days, and I will cause it to rain upon the earth forty days and forty nights; and every living substance that I have made will I destroy (or blot out) from the face of the earth." This, we believe, includes insects as well as the birds of the air: "Everything on dry land that had the breath of life in its nostrils died" (Gen. 7:22 NIV). The "breathe of life in its nostrils" would eliminate the sea creatures who breathe through gills not nostrils. All of this is a picture of the final judgment. Nothing from this evil and fallen realm will be spared, except the things that God chooses. Forty days or forty months represents the time of judgment, the forty years in the wilderness, forty days in the wilderness for Jesus. Noah was six hundred years old when the flood waters came upon the earth and there was the utter destruction of the face of the earth.

12.7 THE ANIMALS

"And they went into the ark, two by two of all flesh, wherein is the breath of life. And they that went in went in male and female of all flesh, as God had commanded him: and the LORD shut him in" (Gen. 7:15-16 KJV).

The Holy Spirit, fulfilling His task of salvation, hovers over the animal kingdom guiding them into the ark. For those who have a hard time believing this, we should meditate on how Balaam's donkey could talk, and how the ravens could feed the prophet Elijah bread twice a day; all operating in ways contradictory to their natures.

"And it came to pass after seven days, that the waters of the flood were upon the earth."

In the six-Violentlyhundredth year of Noah's life, in the second month, the seventeenth day of the month, the same day were all the fountains of the great deep broken up, and the windows (or flood gates) of heaven were opened (Gen. 7:10-11, KJV).

The terms "the fountains of the deep" and "the floodgates" have a greater meaning than just their natural or physical meaning. It is true that the "fountains of the deep" opened and loosed "fiery jet streams," plume-like fissures jutting out of the ocean floor. These worldwide geysers (volcanoes and subterranean waters) spew out hot and moisture-filled molecules into the atmosphere, wetting and soaking the air until torrents of rain descended (Job 22). This "downpour" is meant to reveal the justice and wrath of God toward an ungodly race of men. These were not mere "drops" of rain falling on the earth, but "buckets" of rain. Hence, no man could look toward heaven without being blasted with the rage of God. "That night, the rain descended without mercy without measure....violently pouring on the heads of the wicked" (Bunyan, 3).

"The same day were all the fountains of the great deep broken up" (Gen. 7:11, KJV).

We are meant to envision the great deep, a form of the bottomless pit, the abyss, the empty plains of non-being. Here we see the floods and torrents, the chaotic swirling waters as indicative of everything foreign to the character of God in his attributes of light, order, and grace. "The deep swallows them up from the face of the earth and carries them away from the face and presence of God. Hell has swallowed up its victims." We are reminded of Judas, who after he had convicted an innocent man, killed himself. He did not kill himself from remorse, but as a sign that death had come knocking at his door to collect the final debt: his soul.

"And the waters increased..." (Gen. 7:17, KJV).

God's judgment had no ears to hear the voice of the ungodly, the voice of the damned. Zechariah 7:14 (KJV) says, "Therefore it is come to pass, that as He cried, and they would not hear; so they cried, and I would not hear, saith the LORD of hosts."

Bunyan says succinctly,

> "...Waters were a type of the wrath of God that in the day of judgment shall fall upon ungodly men. So also a type of those afflictions and persecutions that attend the church: for that very water that did drown the ungodly, that did also toss and tumble the ark about, wherefore by the increase of the waters, we may also understand, how might and numerous sometimes the afflictions of the godly be" (Ps. 3:1; Matt. 7:24). "...and lifted the ark, and it rose high above the earth."

The higher the rage and tyranny of this world goest against the church of God, the higher is the ark lifted towards heaven, the proudest wave lifts its highest. The church is also by persecution more purged and purified from earthly and carnal delights....(Gen. 7:17, KJV; cf. Isa. 54:11-13).

"And the waters prevailed..." (vs. 18).

Though the strength of the arm is great, the horse and the rider are still thrown into the sea. Though they were "mighty men of renown," they did not prevail against the waters just as no man will prevail against the fire and brimstone at the end of the age and the coming of the Lord Jesus.

12.8 AFTER THE FLOOD

The fossil record testifies to the massive destruction of marine life with 95% of the fossil record accounted for by marine creatures. Turbidity, temperature changes, and salinity would have been responsible for this massive death graveyard. If any survived to replant the earth, it was in seed form only; whether embedded in the soil, or floating on mattresses of foliage as in the spiritual principle in which a whole generation died in the wilderness, yet their children could go in. Science, biblical and anti-biblical, recognize that there was a time when the earth was barren. Science says, "...A terrible solitude" came over the face of the earth (Morris, Impact, 134). Yet with these seeds, the signs of life, the Lord renewed the face of the earth day by day as he does today.

The "kinds" of animals led into the ark were true "kinds." This is the largest domain of animals. As an example, "Bear" would be a kind, but, polar, grizzly, brown, and black would be species. Hence, all the speciation of the "kind" bear was not on the ark. Only "Bear" was on the ark. The point is that polar, as well as the myriad of birds we see today, including the penguin and the snow owl, were non-existent in the pre-diluvian world. They exist today as species from the "original" kind brought on board. Who knows what the animal world of Adam truly looked like? We know it today in "seed" form only.

The earth's crust was prepared by the flood for the earthquakes and shifts that we see today in the continental regions. All-natural disasters should remind us that the whole earth is temporary and that the seeds of destruction were sown in it at the Flood. The next destruction will be from fire and brimstone in which the fountains of the deep (the core of the earth) will be revealed in volcanoes and earthquakes (Rev. 16:20). The whole earth will be shaken and ultimately cast into the deep. The windows of heaven will pour down fire as it once did rain revealing God's end-time wrath on disobedient and rebellious people. People will run for the mountains and caves, taking refuge outside of the cities, but anarchy, terror, and self-preservation will turn them against each other.

> *"For by this they willfully forget that by the word of God the heavens were of old, and the earth standing out of the water and in the water, by which the world that then existed perished, being flooded with water. The heavens and the earth which are now preserved by the same word, are reserved for fire until the day of judgment and perdition of ungodly men "(2 Peter. 3:5-7, NKJV).*

Listen to what the Scripture further has to say,

> *And as it was in the days of Noah, so it will be also in the days of the Son of Man: They ate, they drank, they married wives, they were given in marriage, until the day that Noah*

entered the ark, and the flood came and destroyed them all. Likewise, as it was also in the days of Lot: They ate, they drank, they bought and sold, they planted, they built, but on the day that Lot went out of Sodom it rained fire and brimstone from heaven and destroyed them all. Even so, will it be in the day when the Son of Man is revealed (Luke 17:26-30).

12.9 A RAINBOW IN THE SKY

The pledge that God makes to Noah is not only a pledge of enduring stability but also of a restatement of His covenant with Adam. There is a correspondence between the covenant established with Adam and the covenant established with Noah. The flood and corresponding judgment was an end to depravity, and a virtual starting over with Noah. "The rescue of Noah put man, and his world on a threshold of a new beginning"(Dumbrell, 1989:39). To Adam, it was a covenant to "take dominion" of a perfect world. For Noah, it was the same command, but now of a disordered world where all relationships are fractured.

Much attention is naturally focused on the fractured relationships of mankind in this section. Little has been said, however, of the relationships between the animal world and mankind. Why does God change the structure of the world order? God says,

"And the fear of you and the dread of you shall be on every beast of the earth, on every bird of the air, on all that moves on the earth, and all the fish of the sea. They are given into your hand. Every moving thing that lives shall be food for you. I have given you all things even as the green herbs. But you shall not eat flesh with its life, that is, its blood" (Gen. 9:2-4, NKJV).

To Adam, only the grains and vegetation of the earth were to be food. Why does God now allow for flesh-eating? To answer this, we must first ask the question, why didn't God allow it in the first place?

The answer is three-fold. (1) Animals were also possessors of a type of soul-life, i.e., they are considered *nephesh,* enjoying a type of life. Although not self-conscious, they still possess life. (2) Man and animals had a harmonious relationship before the fall. All the animals, including tigers, leopards, and so forth, were considered "domesticated." To eat an animal at this stage would have been tantamount to eating a "pet." Animals not sensing any danger, could not have protected themselves. This leads to the final and major reason. (3) It was not in keeping with the character of God to allow wanton destruction of animal life, without some kind of protection for them. "Dread" provides this limited protection today. After the fall, the harmonious relationship was severed, making many animals dangerous predators.

In the covenant with Noah, we see the abiding nature of God's grace. God in his perfect sovereignty works with the free will of man. Despite the choices, man has made. God will overcome.

So history begins its ebb and flow and only those with understanding can follow its outline.

Discussion Questions

1. Explain how the mark of Cain was a pledge from God. What did it signify to Cain and his descendants? How did they corrupt God's word?

2. Discuss with yourselves the idea of the "land of Nod" and how its inhabitants resemble mongrel dogs?

3. The "city habits" produced what works? What drove people to work?

4. The names of both lines signify what chief differences between them?

5. Defend the thesis that the sons of God were not angels. Why not

Bibliography

Bunyan, John. http://christianbookshelf.org/bunyan/the_riches_of_bunyan/xxi_the_church.htm

Douglas, Robert, Ed. *New Bible Dictionary.* Grand Rapids: Wm Eerdmans, 1962.

Dumbrell, W. J. *Covenant and Creation.* Grand Rapids: Baker Book House, 1984.

Fuller, Dan. *The Unity of the Bible*. Grand Rapids: Zondervan Publishing House, 1994

Jamieson, Robert. A.R. Fausset, and David Brown. A Commentary Critical, Experimental, and Practical on the Old and New Testaments. Grand Rapids: Wm. Eerdmans, 1995

Made in the USA
Middletown, DE
19 October 2022